*to Declan, James,
Matt, Michelle, Marley,
Pat, Reina,
and Fuckhead (a.k.a. Tony) —*

adoxography
of an
inaniloquent ~~aeolist~~

(A-hole-ist)

*You're family now.
Tough shit.*

159 sincere apologies, life lessons,
and pseudointellectual observations
(among other things)
by christopher campbell

*Sincerely and Truly
Yours,*

adoxography ***n.*** fine writing on a trivial subject

inaniloquent ***adj.*** full of empty or idle talk

aeolist ***n.*** a pompous person, pretending to have inspiration or spiritual insight

contents.

an author's note.

This book is the culmination of years of hard work and heartbreak. Take everything as you will, but know that I am prone to fits of hysteria, depression, and extreme exaggeration.

That being said, everything you are about to read is completely truthful.

one. entropy saves.

i can feel my breath
in my hands
as my face sits still
waiting for me to
make
my
next
move

seven cans
in front of me
motionless
empty
reminding me why i'm up so late
fucking caffeine
i just don't know how to quit you
and frankly my dear
let's fucking keep it that way

i ache
in silence
both literally
and metaphysically
this silence is *killing* me
just like everything else in life
it's fucking cliché to say
but everything is just killing us slowly
fucking entropy
if you can't beat 'em

wait 'til they slowly decay with time
time heals all wounds
what they don't tell you
is that time heals those wounds with **death**

i bang my head against my keyboard
literally
mostly literally
trying to *inspire* my brain to write
here's to my eighth can
hopefully it'll be my last
(but let's face it, we both know it won't be)

watching the clock
is only making this more painful
as the minutes tick tock away
every muscle in my body tenses
i've got to get out
i'm going insane
i can feel it
i see it when i close my eyes
hear it with each tick tick tick of the clock
the existential dread sets in
and it becomes clear
there's no going back

oh well
i quite like it here
(besides
with all these voices
at least i'll never be lonely)

two. "do you ever run out of things to write about?"

every now
and again
i get asked
if i'll ever run out of
things to say
to which my answer is
yes
obviously
why do you think
hollywood has a hard on for reboots
but sometimes
i do wonder
if that day
will ever come
for me
and then
i realize
as long as
my heart beats
my blood pumps
my mind races
and every part of me
thrives
for love
i will always
have plenty
to fucking complain about

three. love is cancer (us).

sometimes
when it's
dead quiet
i stop to listen for awhile
and when i do
i can hear
the tobacco
in my cigarette
burning
slowly
and it is in that moment
i close my eyes
and pretend
it's my heart

love is cancer (us)
in a way
it frees you
opens your heart
makes you do
crazy things
and slowly
but surely
kills you from the inside

that's love
easy to get
always harder
to get rid of it

you're one
big
fucking
mess
("fucking pathetic")
in like
in love
in lust
infatuated by thoughts of
masochism
nihilism
and me
one fucked up little boy
("could you be any more
fucking
confusing?
fucked up
in that
empty little
head of yours")
perhaps the answer
lies with her
to her
and *next* to her
in her bed
keeping her warm at night
while you
lie alone
dreaming of her

speaking of lying
whatever happened to
good, old-fashioned
fucking
the kind of
fucking
that makes you want to
smoke a cigarette
("you miss that kind of
sex
don't you")
lie to me
lie to her
lie to yourself
it won't make a
goddamn difference
because in the end
when all is
said and done
it'll just be
one more thing
to take with you
to your grave

("and we're all looking forward to that")

five. dance monkey dance.

don't listen to what they say
it's all just pinko commie *bullshit*
that or something closer to the truth
semantics, really
the more you listen to what they say
the more you become the monkey
and they become the man with the music box
the more they play their music
the more you want to dance to their infectious tune
that may be fine for awhile
but you have to start dancing to your own tune eventually
strike up your own beat
take a chance and dance
dance monkey dance
to the beat of your own heart
you just never know what will happen
you might end up happier than you were
you might end up finding another monkey to dance with
an *awesome* monkey
an attractive, charismatic, intelligent monkey
who the music man was trying to keep you from
because he knew you'd love *that* heartbeat more
since the music man was just jealous *he* couldn't have that
other monkey
and now you have that other monkey
you have that other, *awesome* monkey
and fuck a duck if you're not happier that way
(i know i am)

six. death of a subwayman.

the sting of love
strikes blindly at whoever is naive enough to get struck
and *boy* do I feel sorry for *those* guys
you came into this world alone
and that's exactly how you'll fucking leave
nobody there to hold your fucking hand
nobody there to tell you you're off to a better place
just the cold and the dark and the thought of being alone

they say your life flashes before your eyes
and that you see the people you love
but the truth of the matter is
when that subway train hits you
or that shark bites into your leg
or the doctor tells you how long you have left
you don't really see anything at all
you just sort of space out for awhile
you walk around on autopilot
everything loses its color and its meaning
you feel lost, directionless
and you can't seem to focus on anything
there's no flash
there's no retrospective insight

okay, there is *one* thing you do see:
how meaningless life is

nihilism
try it some time

seven. forward it is.

when
the sun
sets
it seems to
break down
any walls
you keep up

and when
the sun sets
your heart sets too
doesn't it

i hate it

there isn't much
you can really
do about it
except
cry
all fucking night long

wait
that's bullshit
you're better off
just letting things go
even if
letting go
is the hardest thing to do

"it hurts
but
it's worth it"

learned that from
satan's lullaby
aka
rock'n'roll

but
in the end
there's
only one
direction
you can go
from here

i'll let you know
when i get there

reality
isn't always kind
sometimes
it takes a dose of
fiction
to touch your heart
and sometimes
you need a few
made up german words
to remind you
what is *most* important in life
i used to think that
loving someone was enough
perhaps for some people
love *is* enough
but i've found that you can love someone
who isn't the best fit for you
it takes more than love
it takes effort
see
sometimes we think we have what we want
we have the thing that is almost the thing that what we want
but not quite
what we truly want
what we truly *need*
is our
lifelong treasure of destiny

nine. masochism, nihilism, and one fucked up little boy.

there wasn't much left for me
but the empty shell of myself
standing in front of a mirror
lonely, with that ringing in my ear
staring at an apathetic shell
that's nihilism for you

but it isn't as hopeless as it seems
(except when you care for someone
when you love someone
and they don't love you back
then you're fucked)

so you lock yourself away
and don't let anyone else in
maybe it's because you fear
that you may just fall in love
with some other poor soul
or maybe you don't want to lose
the memories you've shared with her
either way you're dooming yourself
to a partially unlived life

but maybe you like that
you fucking masochist
you like denying yourself
the pleasures that come with
living your life to its fullest
(how sad)

but that's just it, isn't it
that's just it
you couldn't be anymore *fucked*
than you already are now
(how pathetic)

so do what i could not
let yourself live
let yourself live a life full of love
give yourself to the whims of love
allow yourself to just do whatever the fuck it is
that you *know* you love to do
be whoever the *fuck* you want to be
give no fucks
have no qualms
show no mercy
and give no quarter
(but, you know, as it applies to normal, everyday stuff)

and when it comes to her
just remember two simple words:

(PLACEHOLDER)
(WRITE SOMETHING PROFOUND LATER)

ten. that morning after smell.

all i can do
is stand here
and stare at my
bed sheets
they are
one
big
fucking
mess
all thanks
to a girl
whose name
i never got
sweat
sex
alcohol
and her
mango shampoo
that's all
i can smell
in other words
all i smell is
the morning after

sometimes i feel as if i'm that guy
that guy who shows up to the surprise party late
and when he enters everyone yells surprise
thinking that *he's* the birthday boy
but then they realize he's *not* the birthday boy
so everyone rushes to reset everything
and just when everyone is taking their place
the birthday boy arrives early and ruins the surprise

everyone blames that guy for ruining the surprise
but what nobody seems to remember
is that the person who invited that guy
told him to *be there* at nine
but failed to clarify that the *surprise* was at nine
and that he needed to be there *before* nine
so he showed up when he was told

but nobody cares about semantics
they only care about the fact that he ruined the surprise
so nobody in that group invites that guy to parties anymore

(yeah i'm *that* guy)

twelve. soulless morning pancakes.

these days fly by so goddamn fast
it's hard to keep track of time
or anything, really
when the soul gets lost
in the faded memories
of love, sex, and the morning after
the morning after
what a joke
there isn't much of a morning after
not together
nobody ever remembers much of the morning after
it's just a blurred memory
the color of the sheets you'll never see again
the smell of the pancakes you'll never eat
the complicated contraptions on the door usually intended
to keep people out
but today it feels like they were always meant to
keep people in
sixteen different goddamn locking mechanisms
gone are the front-door-unlocked days
the andy griffith days
because that's the brutal world we live in now
a world where people need sixteen goddamn locks
but can't remember a damn thing from the morning after
(unless of course
you're like me
and you're the one who woke up alone)

thirteen. "how'd you like your metaphor?" scrambled.

"it'll only ever be an egg
a plain, organic egg from USDA-approved all-natural
grass-fed chickens
nothing special"
that's what they said
no—
that's what they *thought*

that plain egg
oblong, smooth
plain as bread
or plainer
it looks as though
it could pass for quaker
but it wouldn't
and it can't
it shouldn't
so it won't

it sat there
and stared
"make me something special
i *want* to be something special
i *can* be something special
i *am* something special"

and boy, let me tell you
i have never enjoyed scrambled eggs so much in my life

have you ever had that feeling
when you run into someone at the market
that you knew them from somewhere
but couldn't really place them
you stop them and ask them where you know them from
they tilt their head because they're as confused as you are
you swear up and down you know them
but you just can't place them
maybe from the coffee house
maybe from the night club
maybe from the book store
or maybe you just know them
because you went home with them
and while they were in the shower the next morning
you grabbed your shit and you left
you didn't say goodbye
you didn't leave a note
you walked out the door
without a word
and the reason they don't recognize you
is because you never once turned the lights on
not a single goddam time
in fact you seem to recall blindfolding her at some point
and there were feathers and whips involved
and now here you are
standing face to face with a woman you burned
probably in more ways than one
"sorry, you just have one of those faces"
man that was a close call

fifteen. bastard bananas.

the other day i bought some bananas
and high holy hell
when i opened my first one
it was brown and mushy
what
the
fuck
it wasn't even brown on the outside
bastard bananas
next time you buy a bunch of bananas
peel one in the store
you'll be better off
and on the upside
you'll have a little snack while you're shopping
i'm not sure that's completely on the up and up
but i'm pretty sure they won't arrest you for it
although there have been cases of stranger things
happening
then again
it's not like we're in the twilight zone

(are we?)

addendum
if we *are* in the twilight zone
it's probably an episode from the later years
with the terrible writing and the predictable twists

sixteen. time spent, time earned.

life is all about the time you spend
doing all the things you love
(and occasionally things you don't)
it really doesn't get better than that

except sometimes it *does*
because as much as life is about time *spent*
it's about the time *earned*
you spend your time doing the things you love
to earn more time
to continue to do those things
with the people you love doing them with
and you love doing things you love with people you love
(don't you)

but really when you think about it
life isn't just about time *spent* and time *earned*
it's about time *killed*
you spend time doing the things you love
to earn more time to do those things
with the people you love doing them with
only to turn around
and find out
that you have all this time to kill
like all the time you kill
waiting for your stupid fucking doctor's appointment
so you read one of the worst books ever written
and you ask yourself why
why

20

and then you remember
you're a writer
you have to read as much as you can
comes with the craft
even if it means
reading popular books that have no literary merit
because
you can't go around
criticizing a book you've never read
just like you can't criticize music you've never heard
or movies you've never seen
so you kill all that fucking time
by reading that stupid fucking book
a book that, after you read it
makes you feel more dumb
dumber
(see)

but after you kill all that time
you realize that you spent time doing something you love
despite a net loss of brain cells
and you gain a whole new appreciation for literature

time *spent*, time *earned*, time *killed*
really that's what life is
that's what the world revolves around
that or the sun
always was a little fuzzy on the details
(maybe that's the ~~alcohol~~ caffeine talking)

seventeen. an orange notebook.

"i set out to find a rhyme for orange
but all I could think of was door hinge
unless you've heard of the mountains of Blorange
in which case you're a fool"

and for a brief moment
i glimpsed
the brilliance of that most worn and beaten
orange notebook
it sat there on the floor
i could feel its pain
years of abuse
expressed openly upon the pages within
the anguish of grief
the sadness and agony of loss
the fear and the hatred and the longing
i could feel it all, all at once
and it was
overwhelming
to say the least
all of it, held slovenly together
by a single, thin, rusting wire
and encased by a fading, tattered, yet somehow brilliant
orange cover
i suppose it is only proper
that the cover of that notebook be
orange
one of the few words in the english language
that simply doesn't rhyme

eighteen. imagine the following written on a legal pad.

sometimes
i challenge
myself
to find
new and
exciting
places
to write
in an
attempt
to be
profound
like the
margin
of a
legal pad
and
sometimes
surprisingly
i make it
work
unless
i were
to write
something
like
metham-
pheta-
mine

nineteen. on the prerequisites for being a writer.

i am often asked
what it takes
to be a writer
and in the past
i never knew
what to say
but i think now
a good response
would be
that feeling
you get:
your body
too tired to move
your brain
won't slow down
won't shut off
the voices
asking you
begging you
to tell their story
your body says
sleep
your mind disagrees
you're torn
being pulled in
multiple directions
that's what it takes
to write
(to write well)

daffodils
outside my window
rocking side
to side
in the breeze
drifting by
ever softly
making its way
into my room
i feel like
a daffodil
wrapped up
in this cool comfort
i close my eyes
slowly
and wish
i never want to leave this place
(ireland)
but all things pass
and so will this
though for some
odd reason
i feel like a part of me
will never leave
and hopefully
dad
neither will that part of you
here's hoping

it's pain
it's anger
it's constant misery
everything reminds you of them
the littlest things
unrelated things
when you lose someone
you see them *everywhere*
for a time
or maybe that's just me
thinking of what he'd say
what he'd do
whether he would laugh
or criticize
thinking of the things
he's missing out on
the things
he always wanted to do
places he always wanted to go
people he always wanted to meet
with all this comes the realization that
you're doing these things
going to these places
meeting these people
watching these movies and
laughing and crying and
why the fuck am *i* so special
what makes *me* so special
that *i'm* still here

getting to experience all these things
and he's fucking *gone*
what lotto did *i* win
huh
which straw did *i* draw
answer me
you fucking cunt
if you're so fucking all-knowing
and all-powerful
and all-whatever the *fuck*
answer me
why am i here
and he's not
that's not fucking fair
if this is your doing then
fuck you
fuck you and all your finger wiggling miracles
and your *good book*
and all your zealots and their righteous hatred

look
if you're real
and part of you was human once
you'll understand my pain
and my anger
and you'll also understand
why i'll never forgive you
and why
i'll never forgive myself

twenty-two. and the stages of.

if one thing can be said
about the aftermath
of losing someone
let it be this:
nothing
in this world
can prepare you
for the loss
of someone
you
love
yet
people ask
why nobody teaches us
what to do
when someone dies
i get it
we all want to know
what to do
it's difficult
it's the most difficult thing
you might ever have to do
but the unfortunate truth is
there just isn't anything
that can be said
there's nothing
that can be taught
just
nothing

just
loss
and grief
and the
painful realization
that you'll
never
ever
hear them tell you
they're proud of you
you'll
never
ever
feel them hug you
after a rough day
that's just how it is
there's no playbook
there's no grieving for dummies[1]
all you can really do
is accept things will never be the same
and do the best with what you have, where you have it

---

[1] *there* is *a grieving for dummies*
and while i respect their effort
it was as if they hired a bunch of writers
who had never actually lost loved ones
and just told them
to imagine what they'd do if their cat died

twenty-three. a river in africa.

denial feels *so good*
someone once said
and i took it to heart
and ever since
i play a little game
that i like to call
american politics
i go around
and deny everything

i've found that
if you deny things
people just assume
you did them anyway
so what's the point
in denying things
like
in movies
when the wife is murdered
they always look at the husband
and when he denies it
he just looks more guilty
but does he *really* look more guilty
or is that just society's way
of reminding everyone
that *nobody* is innocent
because
everyone is guilty of *something*

which is why i invented another game
this one i call
act like you know everyone's deepest, darkest secrets
which will make them self-conscious around you
they'll second guess everything they say and do
begin to psychoanalyze their behavior around you
thinking that they've been giving themselves away
gets 'em *every* time

guilt is a powerful tool
one that is easily abused
you can easily abuse it
without even knowing
so it's best to avoid guilt
and stick with positivity
simply embrace
whatever it is you feel guilty about
because *fuck everyone else*
guilt trips are shitty
and only lead to
women crying after sex
don't be a crier
but more importantly
don't be *that* asshole
that makes people cry
nobody likes that fucking guy
fucking asshole

twenty-four. i'm not angry, i'm disappointed.

fuckfuckfuckfuck				fuck	
fuckfuckfuckfuck				fuck	
fuck				fuck	
fuck				fuck	
fuck				fuck	
fuckfuckfuck				fuck	
fuckfuckfuck	fuck	fuck	fuckfuck	fuck	fuck
fuck	fuck	fuck	fuck	fuck	fuck
fuck	fuck	fuck	fuck	fuckfuck	
fuck	fuck	fuck	fuck	fuck	fuck
fuck	fuck	fuck	fuck	fuck	fuck
fuck	fuckfuckfuck		fuckfuck	fuck	fuck

fuckfuckfuckfuck				fuck	
fuckfuckfuckfuck				fuck	
fuck				fuck	
fuck				fuck	
fuck				fuck	
fuckfuckfuck				fuck	
fuckfuckfuck	fuck	fuck	fuckfuck	fuck	fuck
fuck	fuck	fuck	fuck	fuck	fuck
fuck	fuck	fuck	fuck	fuckfuck	
fuck	fuck	fuck	fuck	fuck	fuck
fuck	fuck	fuck	fuck	fuck	fuck
fuck	fuckfuckfuck		fuckfuck	fuck	fuck

fuckfuckfuckfuck   fuck
fuckfuckfuckfuck   fuck
fuck   fuck
fuck   fuck
fuck   fuck
fuckfuckfuck   fuck
fuckfuckfuck   fuck   fuck   fuckfuck fuck   fuck
fuck   fuck   fuck   fuck   fuck fuck
fuck   fuck   fuck   fuck   fuckfuck
fuck   fuck   fuck   fuck   fuck fuck
fuck   fuck   fuck   fuck   fuck   fuck
fuck   fuckfuckfuck   fuckfuck fuck   fuck

fuckfuckfuckfuck   fuck
fuckfuckfuckfuck   fuck
fuck   fuck
fuck   fuck
fuck   fuck
fuckfuckfuck   fuck
fuckfuckfuck   fuck   fuck   fuckfuck fuck   fuck
fuck   fuck   fuck   fuck   fuck fuck
fuck   fuck   fuck   fuck   fuckfuck
fuck   fuck   fuck   fuck   fuck fuck
fuck   fuck   fuck   fuck   fuck   fuck
fuck   fuckfuckfuck   fuckfuck fuck   fuck

twenty-five. the bargain bin at wal-mart.

a lot of people
have nothing but negative things to say
about wal-mart
why all the hate
i mean besides poor labor practices
and shipping jobs overseas
and you know
all the *actual* negative things
the company does
but i have to tell you
i got like *ten* movies for five dollars the other day
and they may not be cinematic masterpieces
they may not be classics
to be revered for generations to come
but i don't care what anyone says
films like
the matrix revolutions
tansformers: dark of the moon
the happening
shazam
battlefield earth
that conan the barbarian remake with khal drogo
these are quality moves my friends

i couldn't even *type* that with a straight face

twenty-six. depression.

let's take a moment
to talk openly
about depression
we don't talk
about depression
often enough
if you ask me
it's a tough topic
to discuss openly
there's this unspoken fear
a completely normal fear
of being insensitive
but trust me
an insensitive discussion
is better than
no discussion at all

have you ever felt so depressed
you couldn't bring yourself to get out of bed
it's crippling
and to think
there are people who don't believe
depression is a real thing
depression is a vicious, painful illness
one that strikes silently
it can fester over many years
or manifest overnight
it's been misdiagnosed
and for a long time

outright ignored
and it's time for that to stop
it's time for us to acknowledge this illness
depression is a *very real thing*
it's real and it's terrible
no, you can't just suck it up
no, you can't just smile and feel better
you can't cure PTSD with a smile
you can't cure bipolar disorder with a smile
you can't cure depression with a smile
it takes a real fight
real effort
it takes a real support system
and in some cases
real medication
but remember
it all starts with a conversation
whether it's this one
or the one you have with your parents
or your friends
awareness is the first step

but seriously
how could you not see that it's a real illness
i guess if you don't care to look beyond the surface
if you're the type of person that thinks
"if you're depressed just watch a comedy movie"
if you're the type of person that thinks
"there's nothing to be sad about"
i guess i could see how you might think that way
but i also guess that

you're a fucking cunt
depression is **real**   .
it's a real thing
it's a real illness that people suffer from
that warrants treatment
that people fucking die from
but you know what
you're right
i bet that kid with cancer
will suddenly stop having cancer
and feel all better
after he watches patch adams
yup that's a real thing
except *fuck you, you idiot*
that's not how the world works
that's not how *anything* works
as much as we would all love
to stop being sad and be awesome instead
that's not how it works

so the next time you're depressed
the next time you're in bed
barely able to move
tortured by your own mind
and someone says
"turn that frown upside down"
you have my permission
to punch that cunt in the face
and then say
"your face doesn't hurt that bad, just get over it"
that's called turning the tables

it might also be a very rudimentary form of
poetic justice
that or it's late and
my idea of poetic justice
is simplistic and possibly wrong

but more on point
to those of you who are depressed
you **are** worth it
you **are not** alone
and at the very least
know this:

;

twenty-seven. expectance.

when all is said and done
and the dust settles
and the smoke clears
there will be one
and only one
truth
and that is
life is shit
once you accept this
everything else will fall into place
it may not be the nicest truth
or the easiest
but it is what it is
and there's no changing it
life sucks
and then you suffer
you suffer and then you die
and you're forgotten
and that's it

so here's an idea:
accept that life is shitty and unfair
and doesn't play by the rules
and then realize
neither should you
break those goddamn rules
do whatever the fuck you want
expectance is frowned upon

he reaches
into his
pocket
searching
frantically
to find
the last thread
between what's real
and what isn't
he struggles
he sweats
he panics
but he finds it
he has control
that comforts him
at least a bit
at least for now
it just isn't the same
anymore
which only means
trouble
but for now
his sights are set
his eyes are open
but dozens of those around him
their eyes are closed
because his lack of control
his grip on reality slipped
and the only way to get it back

was to take it from someone else
fucking *cunt*
fucking *stupid crazy cunt*
why did you have to go and shoot people
you fucking *fucked up cunt*
maybe
if there's a next time
all of us should take the time
to help people who have lost control
maybe
we should help them
take back their lives
give them a sense of stability
and maybe
we should stop perpetuating violence
and stop allowing people to believe
violence solves problems
gun violence isn't solved by more guns
crime isn't solved by more crime
though sometimes fire is solved by more fire
like when firefighters set control fires
to burn away certain areas
to prevent the bigger fire from spreading
i guess maybe that makes a certain kind of sense

but also
maybe
we should stop letting crazy cunts buy guns

hey it's just an idea
don't shoot the messenger

twenty-nine. moving on.

once you hit
crazy cunts with guns
not many places you can go
hard transition is what i'm saying

but that's a lot like day to day life
hard transitions
nothing is as easy as
say
george lucas scene wipes
everything is choppy
fully of editing errors
and jumps randomly from one shitty event
to another equally or somehow shittier event
just a series of fuck ups
one after another
until finally
one of us gets it right
and then we praise them
hold them high
we smile and laugh and celebrate with them
we revere them as heroes

oh wait
no
we don't do that
we reblog some sappy article on facebook
and then promptly forget about them
while we worry whether or not our photo

got more likes than kaley's photo
because fuck her that dumb slut
always taking pictures in her bikini just to get likes
ugg
(so *that's* how those boots got their name)

that reminds me
what is that thing
with two wheels
that thing you stand on
with the handlebars
and you lean forward
and then it propels you forward
what is that damn thing called
it's not a scooter
this one has a motor
it's like those hoverboards
except it has handle bars
damn what is that thing

something
new
though strangely
something
familiar
it's
different this time
it always is
but this
is different
you
are different
i
am different
it's new
and exciting
exhilarating
(that's a good word
i should use that word more often)
my heart beats
faster
my mind drifts
slowly
into a dream
of you
and me
together
(at last)

it's funny
to know i've felt
something
similar
before
but somehow
i know
it's different
you
are different
and it's the best
damn
feeling
in the world

let's go
the world is waiting
for us
we'll go
together

shall we

fuck
fuck
fuck
shit
fuck
fucking
fuck
goddamn
heartbreak
stupid shit
fucking
hurts
shit
shit
shit
fuck
motherfuck
motherfucking
hell
goddamn
stupid
shit
lying
cheating
goddamn
fuck

breakups suck

thirty-two. i've got a quick turnover rate.

you smiled
i melted
i couldn't help it
i smiled back
how i ever expected
to resist
i have no fucking idea
i was foolish to think
those icy blue crystals
you have for eyes
those beautiful
clear skies for eyes
wouldn't kill me where i stood
fucking sappy, i know
but sometimes you just can't get around the truth
i don't know how you do it
but i enjoy it
very much
now
to win your heart
to sweep you off your feet
a grand gesture of chivalry and romance
where to start

do you think they make a romance for dummies?
(i bet even writers with fake dead cats
could woo a girl better than me)

thirty-three. dollar vinyl.

hello there
mister vinyl record
that i paid
one dollar for
one single dollar
a dollar
to follow
the rise
and fall
of
ziggy
fucking
stardust

and how could i forget
the fucking spiders
from
mars

i can hear
the music
i can see
bowie in space
with a
bedazzled spacesuit

i got laid to this album
listening to that
far out rock

the perfection of
bowie's vocals
and some bullshit story i made up
about how i jammed with
the master of the universe himself

and although i don't have a record player
and i'm forced to listen to this album on cd
i'll watch as you
my one dollar vinyl
lean quietly
and gently
against the rest of my record collection
collecting dust

my apologies, mister ziggy
(i need a day job)

one last thing
before i go
anybody else starting to get the feeling
that bowie was holding the universe together
and that now he's gone
bless his perfect soul
the universe is just going to shit before our very eyes
(thanks tumblr)

thirty-four. a gentle reminder.

just a gentle reminder
you are not alone
you have this book
and you have me
even if you don't know
who i am
and i don't know
who you are
you'll always have the thought
of someone caring
even if it's simply
just another character from a book

sometimes
they make the best companions anyway
a book will never leave you
a book will never reject you
a book will never tell you you're worthless
books will always be there
and so will this one
it will always be there for you
so whenever you need someone
to talk to
to listen to you
just pick up this book
and read
and i promise you
i will be there

thirty-five. a keen observation, oversimplified.

sometimes
people
spend
too much
time
trying to
live their lives
that they
forget to
live their lives

thirty-six. pick-up sticks.

here
i am
on the
edge of
existence
lost
in my
own
head
standing
in a
haze
of
cigarette
smoke
and ash
filled with
regret
and
irish whisky
i've found
that
most things
are
irrelevant
(much like
the title
of this piece)

thirty-seven. dicks.

this world is full of
dicks
good dicks
and
bad dicks
small dicks
tall dicks
red dicks
blue dicks
the kind of dick that takes up two parking spots
and
the kind of dick that puts an empty milk carton back
fucking savages, i tell you
but truthfully
i'm okay with those dicks
i can live with the dicks that don't use their turn signals
or cross the double yellow line on the road
i can live with the dicks that bite into a sees candy but put it
back when they taste the coconut
what i can't live with
what i *refuse* to live with
are the kind of dicks that shoot up public places
the kind of dicks that shoot unarmed black men
the kind of dicks that make women fear going out at night
or the kind of dicks that prevent a trans woman from using
the women's bathroom
that's the correct fucking bathroom, you asshat
she's a fucking woman
complete fucking savages, i swear

thirty-eight. can't see straight.

your kiss
i taste it
in my dream
you're there
i taste you
and
your hair
flowing
across my face
as i rest
my head
on your shoulder
we kiss
do you taste it
it's all a blur
"we're
perfect"
i said
she smiled
a perfect smile
and
reality
seemed
irrelevant

thirty-nine. intertwined.

dark are
the skies
i welcome
the gloom
it's cold
and it's calm
and i wish
i were
with you
at least
the water
is placid
the trees
stand guard
protecting
perfection
but only
at first glance
did it seem
to be so
because soon
i realized
you're
nowhere in sight
far from
intertwined
the way
we used to
be

forty. my biggest fear.

i'll tell you
my biggest fear
if you promise
to keep it
a secret

promise

pinky promise

okay
here it goes
my biggest fear
is
spiders

okay okay
my *actual* biggest fear
is pouring my heart out to someone
having that someone pour their heart out to me
and then the next morning
they wake up
and change their mind

"listen"
"about last night"
not great words to wake up to
worst words to wake up to
besides "your dad isn't breathing"

forty-one. you never know.

i used to spend a lot of my time
trying to figure out what other people were thinking
and how other people felt about me
and it was
exhausting
and a big fucking waste of my time

people are confusing

instead
spend your time
trying to figure out
what *you* are thinking
and how *you* feel about you
because that's *way* more important

be sure of yourself
your thoughts
your feelings
your strengths
and your weaknesses
everything else
well
everything else
will still be just as fucking confusing
but at least you'll know you aren't the problem

that's what matters
right?

forty-two. six by nine.

there are two types of people in this world
there are two types of people in this world
first there are normal people
first there are normal people
they count from one to ten and so on and so on
they count from one to ten and so on and so on
life is simple and linear to them
life is simple and linear to them
they wake up, go to work, make friends, fuck their partners
they wake up, go to work, make friends, fuck their partners

and then there are those people
and then there are those people
the fucking nutjobs
the fucking nutjobs
the weirdos
the weirdos
the all-around whacked out crazy fucks
the all-around whacked out crazy fucks
who count from one to ten and then throw in some letters
who count from one to ten and then throw in some letters
for good measure
for good measure
eight, nine, ten, a, b, c, eleven
eight, nine, ten, a, b, c, eleven
those people who see beyond the line
those people who see beyond the line
outside of the parameters
outside of the parameters

58

i like both kinds of people
i like both kinds of people
sometimes i fall in line
sometimes i fall in line
other times i am thirteen steps ahead
other times i am thirteen steps ahead

but the one main difference between the two
but the one main difference between the two
between the average people and the weird ones
between the average people and the weird ones
between the base tens and the base thirteens
between the base tens and the base thirteens
the average person won't understand
the average person won't understand
even though i repeated it twice
even though i repeated it twice
but the nuts will see why the title of this piece is redundant
but the nuts will see why the title of this piece is redundant
and they'll find meaning
and they'll find meaning
in answers
in answers
without questions
without questions

forty-three. elizabeth barrett browning, a hacky sack, and
some noodles with sliced pineapple.

mystery
it's an important part of life
the pull of the unknown
the anticipation of discovery
the desire for answers

but you would do well to remember
that the power of mystery
comes from not knowing
(that's kind of the whole point, you see)

they say knowing is half the battle
why only win half the battle
winning half of something is not winning
fifty percent is still an f in school, isn't it
so if you're not going to win
why spoil the surprise
a little mystery never hurt anyone
(except maybe curious cats i suppose)

but the truth is
the truth is that the truth is always disappointing
it's never as good as what we imagine it might be
we build it up in our minds
we set these impossibly high expectations
and then once we've figured it out
and it isn't what we thought it was going to be
we wish we hadn't figured it out

so please
i beg you
let the mystery live on
don't let the need to know
ruin the excitement of anticipation
you'll thank me later

oh
one more thing
you're probably wondering
"what the fuck does this have to do with elizabeth barrett
browning, a hacky sack, or noodles with pineapple"
and that's exactly it
you don't know
you want to know
but you don't
but promise me one thing
or rather
promise *yourself* one thing
don't google it
because trust me
you'll be sorry you did
(or will you)
it's not nearly as good as you think it is
(or is it)

forty-four. numbers (and life lessons).

someone pointed out
the word eleven
is fucking weird

like
why don't we say
onety-one

probably the same reason
we don't say
twoty-two
or
threety-three
or
fourty-four
wait
that's just it
we don't say *four*ty-four
we say *for*ty-four
and that may not be a huge deal to you
but i think i speak
for every english major out there
when i say
that's a big fucking deal

because remember kids
in life
u can make a difference

forty-five. sapphire weddings and cosmic solidarity.

i've been thinking
(sounds dangerous, i know)
if i ever get married *(again)*
i'll write my own vows
and stress just how important
solidarity is
ride or die, am i right
since we're on the topic
i have a huge lack of respect
for wishy washy people
i guess some people
refer to them as pancakes
because they flip so easy
(but honestly
every pancake i've ever flipped
has been a pain in the ass)
solidarity is where it's at
the kind of solidarity
that forms planets and shit
universe-creating solidarity, ya know
that's the kind of partner i want
we may disagree
and argue over who gets the clear gummy bears
but i want someone who will
no matter what
stick around to have that gummy bear fight
because that's the kind of love
i can stick to
(since gummy bears are so sticky, ya know)

forty-six. palladium and chromosomes.

you might
have something
in common
with someone
but that
does *not* mean
you're compatible
just throwing two things together
makes *not* a good pair
if that were the case
mixing sprite and sierra mist
would be so good
but have you ever tried that
i bet you haven't
because it's fucking disgusting
i tried it
specifically because i wrote this
nobody should ever do that
savages do things like that

and i think my point is
having things in common is nice
but not completely necessary
peanut butter and bananas
are so different
but so good together

i guess what i'm saying is
maybe pick your dates based on more

than similar movie taste
it won't work out well for you
not in the long run
sure you might have great movie nights
you might both end the movie night
by agreeing the movie was good
and maybe trading your favorite scenes
but
in my humble opinion
(my humble *correct* opinion)
the best kind of movie nights
are the ones where you force your significant other
to watch movies you *absolutely love*
and they *fucking hate*
because i think
again, in my humble *(correct)* opinion
good relationships
solid, strong relationships
the kind of relationships worth writing about
are based on tolerance and acceptance
to be able to tolerate their *bullshit*
and accept that they are *fucking wrong*
i could be wrong
but you can't say
it isn't hella fun
to sit and argue with your sweetheart
about whether or not
the prequel trilogy is as good as the original trilogy
or if it's *utter horseshit*
(besides
if that's the worst argument you ever have with them
i think you're doing alright)

forty-seven. ronin.

being single
is sort of like being a ronin
it's lonely
you're masterless
and honorless
you wander aimlessly
trying your hardest
to find someone
someone to pledge your loyalty to
someone to take you in
someone to give you purpose
someone you'll swear to protect with your life
someone you'd live for
someone you'd die for
i'll be honest
i was making this shit up as i typed
but the more i type
the more it starts to make sense
being single
is like being a ronin
so i guess by default
being in a relationship
is like being a samurai
because by the end of it
you want to commit seppuku
and fucking eviscerate yourself

yeah, this worked out well
i think i'll write a book about this shit

one thing i'm guilty of
is trying way too hard
to make my life seem
cinematic
i see these moments
they're unfolding
and i have this tendency
to try and force them to unfold a certain way
i envision certain things happening certain ways
and a lot of the time
other people just don't see my artistic vision
which isn't a bad thing
but is sometimes just hard to work around
like when i met this girl
we'll call her
the girl from tucson
we met online
and she's wonderful
she's just fucking great, man
i'm crazy about her
she's funny, smart
and gorgeous
we snapchat and text
and talk on the phone for hours sometimes
and i just can't help but think
how romantic it would be
if we ended up together
how cute would that be
like, we both just start thinking

after awhile
"i really like this person
like *really* like them
i kind of hope they like me back
and aren't dating anyone else
even though it's kind of crazy
to expect them to feel the same way
since we're so far away from each other"
and then gradually we both let it slip
and we blush
like on skype or whatever
and we both make the conscious choice
not to date anyone else
but we don't tell each other
and we just keep doing this thing
flirting
skyping
and eventually one of us is like
"i *really* want to come visit you"
and the other one is like
"yeah, that *might* be cool"
but we're secretly both *super* excited
and then one of us visits the other
and it's just like **pow**
super romantic and powerful and obvious
and like we both try *really hard* to hide it
because we don't want the other to know how crazy we are
and then finally
at the end of the first night
we're walking around
with our melting ice cream

complaining about the weather in arizona
and it just *clicks*
and one of us lets it slip
and the other blushes
and then we *both* blush
and it's just crazy and we can't keep it in anymore
so one of us says
"i don't even want this ice cream anymore
it's melting and getting all over"
and the other one is like
"it's all over your *face*"
so the other one, being super awkward and sarcastic, says
"maybe you should lick it off then"
and then the other one takes it *super seriously*
like it is now their sworn duty to lick that ice cream off
so then one of us licks the other
and there's this *super* romantic moment
where our faces are super close
almost touching
and we're both smiling
and it would be the perfect time to kiss
but then one of us pulls away all awkward
and breaks that moment
and the other says like
"you're a *terrible* ice cream licker"
but then the other cuts them off
by diving in for the kiss
and the rest
well
you'll have to keep reading, won't you

forty-nine. striking gold on the devil's crossroads.

everyone has a price
this i'm sure of
even if it's a ridiculous price
everyone has a price
some people have low prices
some people will snort salt for five bucks
i don't care about those people
i'm more interested
in the people who claim not to have a price at all
people who claim they wouldn't
say
suck a dick for two hundred million dollars
like
who *wouldn't* suck a dick for two hundred million dollars
i just don't buy it
i do not accept that you are priceless
i believe
deep down
i could break them
which is why
if and **when** i become wealthy
i will revisit all my old friends
who claimed not to have a price
i'll put *real fucking money* on the line
i'll fill several briefcases with two hundred million dollars
(that's just more realistic, assuming standard briefcase size)
and then we'll see who doesn't have a price, warner

fifty. thrifty.

in limerick, ireland
there's a place
called the milk market
lovely place
super fun
(great craic, they'd say)
it's sort of like
a farmer's market
a lot of people there
sell antiques
handmade goods
trinkets, bits, and bobs
it's almost like
a farmer's second hand store
there are also farmers who sell their crops
but more on point
when i was there
i walked the market many times over
searching for souvenirs, of course
but also
searching for something
to fill the hole in my heart
and there
after hours of wandering and pondering
and peering and leering
i found a simple, old compass
in a small wooden case
there was something about that compass
it was pointed right at me

not north
right at me
i picked up the box
and the little old man
who hadn't said a word
spoke softly
with a heavy irish accent
"i carried that compass with me
through the worst times of me life
through pain and suffering
as a rich man and a poor one
i held it close no matter what
'cuz when life was a cunt
i could find me way thru the dark"
and i swear to you now
it was just like in the movies
that old, grizzled man
who had seen some shit
who had lived his life
with no regrets
and then i realized
his accent was so thick
i completely misheard him
and what he actually said was
"i carried that compass with me
through the worst times of me life
through pain and suffering
as a rich man and a divorced one
i held it close no matter what
'cuz when me wife was a cunt
i could find me way to the bar"

fifty-one. employees only or scarlett johansson.

everyone's got a gimmick these days
i'm not saying it's a bad thing
gimmicks are what drive sales
gimmicks can be wildly profitable
but that's as far as the gimmicks should go
gimmicks are for retail stores
or actors trying to find their niche
gimmicks are not for dating
or making friends
you shouldn't need to wear wild outfits
or say outlandish things
or be known as "that guy"
when it comes to socialization
if you rely on a gimmick to make friends
or to attract the attention of someone you like
you're going to be s.o.l.
when that gimmick grows old
or you grow too tired
and the people around you
suddenly start wondering why they even like you
you'll be left cold and alone
and people will see you for who you truly are
an insecure little boy (or girl)
who needs to pretend to be cool to be cool
take it from me
i'm an expert in this field
i pretended to be australian for three years
and what did it get me
well i did get laid a lot

and people often paid my bar tab
come to think of it
maybe this gimmick thing is a good idea
i mean, at the end of the day
when you're lying in bed
or sitting half naked in the backseat of your car
or sprawled out in the bathroom stall
next to smoking hot line-dancing country chicks
in daisy dukes and cowboy boots
you'll feel empty inside
despite the constant attention
despite the adoration of women
and the jealousy of men
you'll feel unfulfilled
because deep down
you'll know that these people
these tan, blonde, blue-eyed goddesses
only like you for your gimmick

okay maybe i should end this here
because i am really starting to struggle
it's becoming harder and harder
to see a downside to this gimmick thing

so yeah
don't do drugs

well, don't do hard drugs
pot is cool

fifty-two. word count.

words, words, words
carefully crafted
are a powerful thing
they paint a picture
without color
they persuade
intimidate
and deceive
they make us laugh
they make us cry
and in the
right amount
arranged in
the right way
they reach out
and touch our souls
remember
words are important
but so is

fifty-three. the love bug.

some people believe in a
love bug
i'm not really one of those people
i guess the idea of a
love bug
as a metaphorical tool for writing
is useful
bitten by the love bug
but i always felt that
love bug
makes it seem like love is some sort of
virus
or venom
something you can catch
or contract
doesn't sound pleasant
but then again
the idea of love doesn't sound pleasant
when you think about it in a big picture sort of way
being in love
you pick one person
and give them intimate knowledge
of how you feel and think
you tell them all your secrets
and let them in
that's like superman giving lois lane kryptonite
i mean, it's lois lane, she ain't gonna use it
but *what if,* man
what if

fifty-four. base thirteen.

a valuable life lesson:
not everything is about love
that has been the hardest lesson to learn
for me at least
because so much of my energy (and money)
has been spent (wasted)
in the pursuit of love (lust)
when in reality
that isn't what we should be looking for
nobody should *search* for love
love is something
that happens gradually with time
instead
we should all try and find happiness
happiness within ourselves
happiness around us
because at the end of the day
happiness is much more satisfying than love
and it comes in many different forms
and the best part about happiness
it won't gangbang five black guys in your apartment while
you're at work

life is full of questions
questions that don't matter in the end
because what really matters
is how you go about answering them

fifty-five. dad.

dad was fifty-five when he passed
he died on my birthday
my twenty-third birthday

the new year was not kind
we had just lost our home
moved out on valentine's day
we were living in a hotel
our entire lives
crammed into a storage unit
we were scraping by
but we were okay
he had raised me right
taught me to appreciate
everything i had
there was hope for us
i had faith in us
our ability to overcome
to succeed no matter what
i had hope
boy was i naive

it was late
i had gone out after work
to celebrate my birthday
must have been almost 5am
when i tiptoed quietly
back into our hotel room
i could hear him snoring

normally when i came home late
i'd wake him up
let him know i was home safe
but that week had been stressful
he needed his sleep
we all did
i didn't wake him
instead i crawled into bed
fully clothed
and passed out

"chris, wake up"
my dad's new girlfriend
shook me awake quickly
i could barely keep my eyes open
i looked at the clock
just past 8am
i still needed sleep
didn't she understand
"something's wrong with your dad"
that's all it took
i was wide awake
"your dad isn't breathing"
fuckfuckfuckfuckfuckfuck
what's wrong
what's happening
i looked over at my dad
both of us still laying down
in our respective beds
and i knew
with one look

he was gone
i knew immediately
he had died
i could see the purple
lividity they call it
it had set in
that only happens
when you've been dead
at least two hours
he had died sometime in the morning
between my entry
and being shaken awake
(later we would learn he passed around 6:30am)
"check on your dad" she said
but i already knew
but i didn't know how to say it
so i leaned over him
and put my hand on his shoulder
cold to the touch
i checked for a pulse
out of habit
she needed to see it
she was hysterical and needed to see it
she ran downstairs to the front desk
to call the police
the paramedics
anyone
anyone who could come save him
but he was beyond saving
i knew that
but she didn't

my memory is a bit hazy after that
at least until my friends started to show up
i remember making a few calls
calling out of work
i remember calling work and saying
"they're taking my dad to the hospital"
(i don't know why i lied
i think i wanted to believe he could be saved)
the girl i was dating
she showed up the fastest
my friends trickled in slowly after that
they put us in a different hotel room
while the paramedics did their thing
and at some point
they brought us up
so we could say our goodbyes
that part i remember
in great detail
there he was
laying on the bed
eyes closed
he looked like he was sleeping peacefully
i almost didn't believe he was gone
but he was pale and cold
i leaned in and whispered something to him
(something i will never repeat to anyone)
i kissed him on the forehead
and i walked out of the room
none of my friends or family would leave me alone
they didn't want me to be alone
not through something so terrible

i spent that whole week with friends and family
they stayed the night in my hotel room
they spent every hour of every day with me
but at the end of that week
when i finally found myself in my hotel room
alone
i reflected on everything that happened
and i cried through the night
but just as the sun was rising
i remembered
the day before my birthday
i was supposed to have rehearsal
but i ended up rescheduling
because my dad wanted to get birthday lunch together
so that's what we did
we had panda express
we both got our usual
we sat and ate and talked for over two hours
and at the end of our lunch
he gave me a present
and he said
**"Times are tough, but you're a Campbell, and you're
my son. No matter what, I'm proud of you. We'll get
through this together. I promise."**
it was a picture frame
with a photo of us
the look in his eyes said
he wished he could have afforded a real gift
but the look in my eyes said
his love and his pride for me were enough
they would *always* be enough

fifty-six. no substitute.

life is unfair
which is fair
because it never claimed otherwise

sometimes i find a nice quiet place
to sit and reflect
i think about all the things that have happened
how they could have been different
but then i remember
that i am who i am today
because of everything that has happened
things happened the way they did
and i am grateful to be where i am
even if part of me still wishes
some things could be different
dad is gone
brian is gone
but neither of them is forgotten

as i write this
i am sitting along the banks
of the river shannon
on a cold, overcast afternoon
i can't help but think
they would have loved this place
and in a way
they're here with me
and even though they're gone
they'll never be forgotten

dad would have been fifty-six that year
there's a lot he missed out on
season finales of his favorite shows
movies he would have loved
in a lot of ways i feel undeserving
to watch those shows and those movies
to experience all these things
that he would have loved
without him here
to share those experiences with

dad used to say
"There's no substitute for experience."
i used to roll my eyes
whenever he'd say it
it's a *dad* thing to say
he said it so much
that i had stopped listening
and i never really took the time
to understand what it meant
but now that i look back
boy was he right
i finally understand
and better appreciate
his fatherly wisdom
there *is no* substitute for experience
and that's comforting to me
to know that he was right
through the good experiences and the bad
nothing will ever be worth more to me
than my time with my dad

fifty-seven. nothing on.

there comes a point
in every adult's life
when opportunity knocks
you find yourself home alone
the curtains are all closed
and you have that thought
"i could walk around naked"
who would stop you
it's your place, after all
nobody else is around
nobody is going to judge you
everybody thinks about it
and i'm more than certain
everybody does it
even if they'd never admit it

so there you are
you fucking champion
standing naked in the middle
of your mostly empty living room
proudly displaying yourself
for nobody *but* yourself
and that's how it should be
you beauty queen, you

just don't forget to turn off the air conditioning

i love living in california
it's a great place to live
for many, many reasons
but for all the things
that make california great
there are little things
little things like
traffic on the 405 during rush hour
traffic downtown
parking downtown
parking in hollywood
traffic in hollywood
traffic in santa monica
parking in santa monica
parking in west la
traffic in west la
come to think of it
traffic and parking in general
anywhere in or around the greater la area
oh and driving while it's raining
not because i find it hard to drive while it's raining
but because californians think they need to drive 15mph
under the fucking speed limit
that's what the treads on your tires are for, you fucks
and while we're on the subject of california
why the *fuck* does everyone put avocados on *everything*
avocados are good
but they're not *put that shit on everything* good
fuck

fifty-nine. opus.

these days
i find myself wondering
if being a writer is worth it
if it's worth all the hassle
all the heartbreak
all the late nights
sitting in front of a computer
wasted away imagining things
rather than doing things
all the cups of coffee
and all the sugar packets
(how i take my diner coffee:
eight sugar packets and two creamers)
is it really worth it all
sometimes i lay around
and imagine what my life would be like
if i had spent the time i spent writing
doing other things
how many instruments could i have mastered
how many languages could i speak
how many countries could i have visited
how many people would i know and love
how many bridges could i have avoided burning
and how many new ones could i have built
if i never wrote that opus

i guess i'll never know
(it's totally worth it)

sixty. buckminsterfullerene.

everyone has that one friend
who they keep around
but they aren't really sure why
maybe they're a hold over
a relic from a time in your life
where you needed someone
who was always there for you
maybe you were once close
but have grown apart over time
maybe you always meant to get closer
but never found the time to do so
but when it comes to deciding
whether to remain friends or not
you get that odd feeling
that you're friends for a reason
you're just not sure what it is
sort of makes you feel like
you'll regret losing this friend
you think to yourself
"one day i might have a need for them"
so you hang on to that friend
you casually reach out and touch base
just about every month or two
until you find a use for them
i call that a bucky ball friend
it *seems* useful
you know you'll need it *eventually*
but as of right now
there's no specific application

sixty-one. straya.

i mentioned earlier
that there was a time
a long time ago
when i pretended to be australian
those were good times
you know
despite what most people said
my accent was on point
and if i'm being honest
i'm still fairly convinced
that all the people
who claim they didn't fall for it
totally fell for it
like, one hundred percent
and now that they know it was all fake
they want to deny being gullible
which i don't understand
i was very convincing
my story was incredibly detailed
like painful so
and i had a fake australian id card
it's not like i simply said "i'm aussie"
and people just went "okay"
(actually that did happen a few times)
on a related note
why is it socially acceptable to change how we look
but somehow not okay to change how we sound
like, it's okay to want to *look* irish with red hair
but the second we try to *sound* irish

everyone tells us to grow up and stop playing pretend
what if i want to sound like that
what if i want to talk like that
why do i have to be from ireland to sound irish
why can't i simply choose how i talk
we choose the words we speak
why can't we choose *how* we speak them
i want a fucking aussie accent
that's how i want to fucking sound
i think i sound fun and entertaining
so i should be able to talk however i want
but *no*
the second you talk with an accent
and someone asks you if you're from there
and you say no
you just look like a fucking crazy person
and speaking of crazy people
i think that's the real appeal of being an actor
you can sound *however the fuck you want*
and when people ask
you can simply say
"i'm an actor"
actors are just socially accepted crazy people
well
socially tolerated

sixty-two. strayan babes.

since we're on the subject
australian women are *beautiful*
it's almost ridiculous
i have an australian friend
we'll call her
my friend from australia
she's *gorgeous*
we met on a penpal website
(which, let me tell you
is a brilliant fucking idea
if you aren't a member
go join one after this)
she became one of my best friends
she's absolutely wonderful
she even sent me a care package
filled with australian goodness
(which reminds me
i still need to send hers)
but the *real reason* i wrote this
is to stress the importance
of experiencing the world
you can do it without spending a fortune to travel
by making friends in other countries
exposing yourself to other cultures
immersing yourself in other languages
experiencing other people from around the world
and what they have to offer
trust me
you won't be disappointed

sixty-three. subtlety.

i've never placed much value
on general information about someone
i'm fairly certain that sounds dumb
without any context
what i mean is
knowing what someone's favorite color is
doesn't mean much
compared to something like
knowing exactly how they like their coffee on rainy days
or knowing which silly voice you do brightens their day
i guess a better way to put it is
the subtleties of your relationship with that person
are what matter the most
you can recite information
remember names and dates
but you can't really put into words
how someone makes you feel
when they look at you just right
and smile in that one particular way
and their nose twitches slightly
and the hair on the back of your neck stands up
because you know they're the one
those subtleties
the nuances of each facial expression
that's the stuff of true passionate love
that's the shit writers dream about
(and sometimes even write about)

sixty-four. who could ask for more.

most writers strive
to write the perfect *something*
the perfect story
the perfect dialogue
the perfect play
i say **fuck it**
nothing's perfect
instead
writers should strive to write *imperfectly*
to best imitate life
that should be the goal
don't bother
indicating precisely what you mean to say
make up words
fuck punctuation
embrace your inner shakespeare
really go to town
drunk, sober, high
whatever
but make sure
above all else
you write from the heart
it will be imperfect
and that's okay
because life is full of imperfections
and it's those imperfections
that make us perfect
(it'll make sense eventually
many years from now)
(when i'm sixty-four)

sixty-five. love affair.

that's my life
a series of love affairs
one after another
sometimes i get the feeling my life would be meaningless
if i wasn't in pursuit of love
the thrill of the first date
the confident, borderline cocky flirting
and the best feeling of them all
the moments leading up to the first kiss
that nervous excitement
mixed with the fear of rejection
mixed with the anticipation of success
it doesn't get much better than that
but all of that having been said
it's time for a confession:
it's hard for me to maintain interest after the first date
it's just so new and exciting, ya know
a new mystery to unravel
a new *first* to experience
maybe that's why i've had so many one night stands
wait
what if it's *me*
what if *i'm* the uninteresting one
and the reason why things never last longer than a month
is a fear of letting people get close only for them to find out
that i am deeply flawed and lacking in substance

nah
i'm awesome

sixty-six. 2,448 miles; or, how i learned to stop hating long
distance relationships and love sexting.

i never understood
why people have so much hate
for long distance relationships
it always seemed so straight forward to me
and in a lot of ways
long distance relationships are more genuine
so many women i know
are worried that guys are only interested in them for sex
but long distance relationships lack physical intimacy
you would think
long distance relationships
would be more common
or at least more socially accepted
long distance relationships promote a more intimate
intellectual and emotional connection
they require more commitment
they focus on more than the physical intimacy
it forces you to talk
to share stories about your everyday life
you yearn to know more about your partner
because you aren't there to experience life with them
that deeper connection
it can be more meaningful
plus
sexting is hilarious *and* fun
and nudes are awesome
who doesn't love nudes

sixty-seven. she loves me (not).

i've got a beautiful
girl
in my life
i stared into her eyes
into what i thought were
wild honey pies
i said
"i've got a feeling
that I have
got to get you into my life"
i want to tell you
what exactly
she said
she said
"oh darling
you better
think for yourself
because
tomorrow never knows
and
i've got to
get back
so
run for your life
and
cry, baby, cry"
so i cried
and she frowned
and she said to me

"i've got a feeling
it'll be
a long, long, long
long and winding road
please don't
wait
run for your life
and
get back
to
what goes on
here, there, and everywhere"
you can imagine
that things are not
getting better
she's leaving home
and i'll just have to
dig it
martha, my dear
please please me
be mine
i me mine
and our love
let it be
just the
two of us
come
together
we can
carry that weight
across the universe

sixty-eight. sex adjacent.

she said
"i dont have the best hair for sex"
so i checked

yup
good to go

"i mean my hair is too long and gets everywhere"
ah
i stood* corrected
*laid (we were in bed)

i did get a strand or two
in my mouth
but hey
it's all part of the experience

but i digress
point is
we had sex
and she didn't even take off her red leather jacket
perfect night

what was i talking about?
oh ya

moral of the story:
this is what happens when you're sure of yourself
(it's all* connected)
*some of it anyway

sixty-nine. yellow umbrellas and blue french horns.

there's this myth
perpetuated by society
that there is one special person
out there somewhere
waiting to fall in love with you
and waiting for you
to fall in love with them
and i think that's just ridiculous
how could we possibly
only fall in love with one person
there are billions of people on the planet
think of how many people you interact with
on a daily basis
think of how many people you've met
how many people you've crossed paths with
how many people you've dated
and are going to date
how in the world
could you ever be expected
to only fall in love with one person
being in love
isn't some exclusive thing
you don't only ever love one person in your lifetime
so with that being said
why can't we be in love
with more than one person at a time
why did we place some imaginary limit
on who and how many people could have our heart
absolutely ridiculous

sometimes you want a yellow umbrella
sometimes you want a blue french horn
and sometimes you want both
a yellow umbrella *and* a blue french horn
you love them both
you love them both equally
and that's normal
that's okay
don't let anyone make you feel bad
for being in love with more than one person
i am in love with a few people
it's not something i can explain
not something i feel the need to explain
i love them
with all my heart
unconditionally
and that's that
i love who i love
each one of them is special to me
i love each of them equally
and if i ever find someone
to be in a relationship with
i will still be in love with who i'm in love with
but i will promise myself in all ways
to only one
so be in love with who you're in love with
the only opinion that matters
when it comes to your love
is yours
fuck anyone who tells you otherwise
(and you thought this was going to be about sex, didn't you)

100

seventy. wishful thinking.

this pillow
that smell
your hair
as i lay
here
arms wide open
eyes wide shut
pretending
you're here

but soon
my eyes
will open
and i'll
realize

this

pillow

will

never

be

you

seventy-one. eleanor.

to me
dating always felt like
well
it felt like being a car collector
on the hunt for that one car
a 1971 sportsroof mustang
eleanor, if you will
the one, perfect car
you've always wanted
but constantly eludes you
you test drive other cars
but deep down you know
it's not a 1971 sportsroof mustang
but car collectors are so picky
they want a 1971 sportsroof mustang
but they don't want just *any* 1971 sportsroof mustang
they want *the* 1971 sportsroof mustang
with a 1973 restyle
and i think that's ridiculous
how often do you come across a 1971 sportsroof mustang
and you're going to
what
pass it up because it's not the 1971 sportsroof mustang
with the 1973 restyle
you're dumb as fuck
good luck finding another 1971 sportsroof mustang
you idiot

seventy-two. it's the thought that counts.

when i'm
old and alone
and somewhere
down the
beaten path
i won't
regret
a thing
because
i won't
really
be alone
i'll have
thoughts
of you
you aren't here
but
i promise
i'll search
high and low
for you
and if
i don't
find you
i'll know
the thought
of you is
right here
in my heart

seventy-three. good little catholic.

why is it
that whenever i mention
i'm an atheist
the first thing
people always ask
is if i was raised catholic
even as a non-believer
i find that offensive
as if there's some
strange correlation
between atheism
and being raised catholic
i mean
i *was* raised catholic
and quite frankly
catholicism is a load
but i'm not an atheist *because* of that
i'm an atheist because it just makes sense
not to mention
it's oddly comforting
thinking there's nothing
especially
because i would absolutely suffer eternally
for the shit i've done
(nonexistence sounds more appealing)

though since we're on the topic
i've always thought hell would be a pretty cool place
especially if rock'n'roll really is the devil's music

she asks
why i still love her
she never got it
it's called
unconditional love
if i stopped
because you stopped
it wouldn't be
unconditional

she asks
why i still hold on
she doesn't get it
i promised her
with all my heart
if i broke it
because you left
it wouldn't be
a real promise

she says
i should let go
she'll never get it
i told her
i won't let go
but what i didn't say
because i couldn't say
is that i won't let go
because i can't let go

seventy-five. brian anderson.

every once in awhile
you meet someone
someone special
who changes your life
in ways
you could never have predicted
those people
are worth more
than any amount of words
i could ever write
his name was brian anderson
he was my best friend
even in his last years
when we grew apart
when his illness tore him
from his loved ones
he always had a place
in my heart
he died the way he lived:
his way
it may be painful to say
but i couldn't imagine
him living
or dying
any other way
it was his life
his to do with as he pleased
and in the end
when his illness took hold

and left him cold and alone
he did what he had to do
to end his suffering
people say
that people who take their own lives are cowards
but not brian
brian was one of the brave ones
he wasn't afraid to be himself
to take charge of his life
even if it meant
taking charge of his death
and though his loved ones
still remain
and are in pain
more pain than you can imagine
we are comforted by the fact
that brian had made peace
with himself
with god
and that
even though it may have been a sin
god would understand
god would understand he was suffering
and we hope
with all our hearts
that he has gone to god
and that god would forgive him
knowing that brian did what he felt
would heal his wounds
and bring him closer
to the one person he loved more than us

seventy-six. a proper eulogy for a proper friend.

you know
come to think of it
the eulogy i gave
at brian's funeral
was terrible
he loved the big lebowski
so i did what he'd want
and i gave the eulogy
john goodman's character
gave for steve buscemi's character
he would have liked that
but it wasn't really complete
there was more i wanted to say
more about him
more about his family
more that i wanted to acknowledge
because in the end
we are what people remember of us
that's what brian would say
and i remember
i remember swimming in his above-ground pool
making water balloons
and throwing them at the neighbor kids
i remember playing basketball
with everyone in his neighborhood
i remember making prank calls
and getting reprimanded by his parents
while we were sitting in his office
taking turns playing n64

i remember our sleepovers
staying up late trading pokemon
and trying to catch the late nite cinemax movies
i remember doing magic shows for our families
being blindfolded with a gimmicked blindfold
and when brian held the watch in front of me
(i was using "psychic powers" to identify the items)
i yelled "too close" and swatted the watch away
giving away the trick
but nobody cared
because they weren't watching our magic
they were watching us
they were watching our enthusiasm
because if it's one thing
brian should be remembered for
it's his enthusiasm

now i understand
it's hard to connect
with someone you've never met
and that reading this
without knowing brian
makes it seem hollow
but i urge you to think of your best friend
or a family member
think of someone who means the world to you
and then you'll understand
you may not know *brian*
but you know the *feeling*
it's universal

when my dad was my age
he made his own movies
he did everything
he wrote them
directed them
starred in them
the main character
was a private detective
al mccord, private investigator
solved crimes
and looked good doing it
had a run in with the mafia
and came out on top

those movies
as campy as they may seem now
they are works of art
they are a reflection of his hard work and dedication
my dad poured his heart and soul into them
if only hollywood
learned to do the same
rather than churn out
remake after remake
and subpar sequels
we could use more people in this world
that pour their heart and soul into everything they do
i guess that's the moral
put a piece of yourself in everything you do
and be proud of the things you do

seventy-eight. a picture's worth.

the one and only time
i've ever had a tarot reading
i was completely shocked
at just how **fucking lame** the whole thing really was
but i sat and i listened
and about the only thing
i took away from the whole experience
was that tarot reading
was no different than religion
they both appeal to the spiritual side of your brain
they both appeal to the desire to better your life
they both can be hopeful and positive
and they can both be frightening and damning
but overall
they're just a tool
a conduit
through which our spirituality can be channeled
and when it is
when we've unlocked that side of ourselves
we see there is something bigger than ourselves
whatever it may be
and we can use that bigger picture
to help ourselves grow
and guide ourselves down a better path
speaking of pictures
at least tarot cards have cool ones
the bible doesn't have any
which is crazy
because there are some wild stories in the bible

most people walk through life
overestimating what they have
they think they have gold
but they don't
they don't take the time to really look at what they have
when what they really have is a big pile of fool's gold
maybe that's enough for them
maybe they're satisfied thinking their fool's gold is gold
they do say ignorance is bliss
but standing on the outside looking in
it's just so unsatisfying
things are what you make of them
but wanting your fool's gold to be real gold
doesn't make it so

some people walk through life
underestimating what they have
they think they're worthless
but they aren't
they don't take the time to really look at what they have
when what they really have is a big pile of gold
maybe that's enough for them
maybe they're satisfied thinking their gold is worthless
they do say ignorance is bliss
but standing on the outside looking in
it's just so unsatisfying
things are what you make of them
but thinking your gold is worthless
doesn't make it so

eighty. vividly.

women come and go
but some women
some women leave their mark
ink stains on your arm
a scar from a butter knife blade
some less visible
a mark on your heart
those are the best
but also the worst
you remember them vividly
every detail
from the way they laugh
to the way they crinkle their nose
when they're pissed at you for leaving a hickey
because now they have to wear a scarf to work the next day
you remember every detail
like the way she ties her shoes
and the look on her face when she tells you
she doesn't love you the way you love her
you remember everything
and you relive it
when you look in the mirror
and see those marks
or when you close your eyes
and hear her calling
in the middle of the night
because she needs you

she doesn't call anymore

eighty-one. fuck metaphors (*and* similes).

whenever i'm on the beach
i always stop to look
for a rock shaped like a heart
more often than not
i never actually find what i'm looking for
but let me tell you
just the other day
i found one
a small heart
that fit perfectly in my palm
so i held it in my hand
i smiled and thought of you
and threw it out as far as i could

i've never been any good at metaphors
like a monkey driving a firetruck
(that was a simile)
but what i *am* good at
are hidden and cryptic meanings
but i'll spell this one out:
(because for the first time
it's worth the effort)
you are the rock
we're a perfect fit
and before you tilt your head
i'm not going to toss you aside
i'm not the man holding the rock
(that's fate)
i'm the ocean

eighty-two. drumroll, please.

sometimes
we have to find joy
in the little things
the fleeting moments
and friendships
people we meet
but grow apart from
sometimes
you meet someone
and you're drawn to them
you share a night
a handful of moments
great moments
and you both
make the promise
to reconnect
sometime in the future
but for whatever reason
you never do
but that's okay
sometimes
people come into our lives
very briefly
but have a huge impact
it's one of the best feelings
in the world
until you part ways
and then
it's utterly heartbreaking

she smiled
i smiled
she laughed
i laughed
her name was paige
she was intoxicating
she drew me
the cutest thing
i couldn't tell you
what it was
the only thing
that stood out
was the
deathly hallows
we spoke
we shared
we connected
and she said the most wonderful things
things i could never do justice
by writing down
but her words
they hit home
and i haven't been the same since
but truly
the weirdest part
of our connection
was that
she was my waitress
and i was on a date with someone else
and to this day
i still feel *terrible*

116

because the girl i was on a date with
she could feel the connection
she watched as paige and i connected
and let me tell you
there is no worse feeling
than watching someone you like
connect with someone else
right in front of your eyes

word of advice
don't take the people
who care for you
for granted
you'll end up
with nothing to show for it
but a soul full of regret
and a napkin of sketches
from a girl
you'll never see again

and paige
if the universe
has a sense of humor
and you're reading this
let's keep things
the way they are:
drumroll, please

she was right
i'm sure she loves hearing that
she was right
and i was wrong
but that's nothing new

having someone
who is there for you
no matter what
and being that someone
to someone
is beyond words
it's not just comforting
it's true comfort
it's not just helpful
it's lifesaving
it's not simply caring
it's love

i love her
though i'm terrible at showing it
even worse at saying it
but hopefully
somehow
some way
she knows
and maybe
she loves me too
(a guy can dream)

eighty-four. the best things in life.

they say
the best things in life are free
but i disagree
the best things in life are unavailable
and when i say things
i mean women
(obviously)
the best women in life
are always unavailable
it's almost as if
there's some universal law
that specifically states
that the best women
the honest
hard working
dedicated
trustworthy
intelligent
talented
star-wars-loving
beautiful-inside-and-out women
have boyfriends
and not even *good* boyfriends
no
they're always with shitty
asshole-ish
deceptively chauvinistic douchebags
that's how the universe works
it's like some cosmic fucking imperative

eighty-five. the giraffe imperative.

look
this may sound offensive
but i'm fucking tired of making friends
i have plenty of friends
i don't need more
i don't make time for my current friends as it is
fuck making time for *new* friends
but here's what i'm getting at
if i meet a girl at a bar
and we talk and we flirt
and we have a strong connection
things are going really well
and then she decides
that the *end* of the night is the opportune moment
to tell me she has a boyfriend
but follows it up with
"but we can still be friends, right"
i reserve the right to simply say *no*
and walk away without seeming like an asshole
that should be a socially acceptable thing
and i'm going to start it
we'll call it
the giraffe imperative
wanting to connect only with someone you intend to date
named after a wonderful woman i met at the bar
who is perfect for me in every way
(excluding the boyfriend part)

120

eighty-six. hope.

these days
it seems like
there is more negativity in this world
more shitty people
doing shitty things
making people feel shitty
and just generally
flooding the world with their shittiness
it's fucking depressing
what's wrong with people
what's wrong with the world
everything's gone to shit
and to be frank
i'm starting to feel like i'm all out of hope for humanity
that's such a shitty realization to have
to think to yourself
i've lost all hope for humanity
but what's worse
is the fact that there are plenty of people
who feel the same way i do
but after they put down this book
they won't even think twice
they'll continue to shit on others
they keep living their shitty lives
and won't do a damn thing to change
and i think that's just the shittiest
to see the problem
and not do
a damn thing about it

that's as shitty
as having caused the shit
in the first place
it's a shitty world we live in
no
it's a *wonderful* world we live in
filled with *wonderful* things
awesome things
it's only shitty because *people are shit*
humans are destroying this world
and what's truly horrifying
is that humans are the only ones
who can save it
and if you're anything like me
you lost hope for humans a long time ago
so instead
find hope in yourself
you're the only one you can rely on
hold the door open for shitty people
treat shitty people well
let shitty people do their shitty things
and live their shitty lives
while you do some good in this world
be good
do good
be kind
do kind(ness)
and maybe
just maybe
things will be *slightly* less shitty
here's hoping

eighty-seven. an honest inquiry, honestly.

i've never been able to put into words
how i really feel about dating
it's such a strange topic for me
sometimes you meet a girl
who you would love to wine and dine
but they're in that stage of their life
where they want zero commitment
and just want to hook up
but like
how do you say
"i'd like to go on a date but if you'd rather hook up
that's okay too"
not really easy to slip into conversation
whenever you say
"i'm down to hook up"
you look like a non-committal chauvinist
but when you say
"i want to date you"
they don't hook up with you because you seem clingy
what a strange paradigm
i'm sure some of you might read this and shake your head
but that's just it
why can't we talk openly about these things
why can't i tell a girl i'm down for whatever she wants
without looking like a sleezy piece of shit

man
staying single and hiring escorts
is *so* much easier than dating

everyone
and
i
mean
everyone
has had a moment
behind the wheel of a car
on the freeway
or that long stretch of road
speeding through the desert
when they look down at the speedometer
and slowly accelerate
reach that
88mph
and shout
to the future
i don't care how old you are
you've done it
everybody has
and if you're reading this
and thinking
"i've never done it"
then
fuck you
you don't deserve to travel through time
you savage

the key to true happiness
truly

you know
i've never really stopped to think about
how celebrities view the rest of the world
we see them as idols
people worth our reverence
but do they think of *themselves* that way
probably not
or if they do
they must be pretty narcissistic
i've always wondered how taylor swift views herself
if she treats the world the same way i would

i like taylor swift
all of my friends are painfully aware of this fact
i *love* her music
and she's been a positive influence in many peoples' lives
including mine
but setting that aside
it would be interesting to see how she really is
outside of the performances and the appearances
to see if she truly is a good person
of course
like many
i've fantasized about befriending her and dating her
and while most of my friends might find it hard to believe
i really couldn't be close to her
if she wasn't truly a good person at heart
it would feel inauthentic
and i'm *nothing* if not authentic

so
if this *is* the twilight zone
and taylor
you're reading this
first off i love your music
it really speaks to me
second
i hope
at the end of each day
when you crawl into bed
you are happy with the person you are
because that is the most important thing
and this goes for every celebrity
the most important thing is that you are happy being you
not what your fans think
not what the media thinks
truly
if you can sit back and reflect on your life
and you can say
in all honesty
that you are no different than anyone else
that you
just like everyone else
have the power to do good and change the world
and you can say
with all sincerity
that you wake up every morning
and do your best to bring hope to this bitter world
then *fuck*
you're way more awesome than i thought
(also you should call me sometime)

126

ninety. unfinished business.

and all the pieces fell together
as we interlocked our lips
i had a girl with snowflake eyes
and beauty on my fingertips
and when those pieces fell together
they fell right out of place
i could feel the girl with snowflake eyes
melting out of our embrace
hope had packed her bags and left
and i lost the will to smile
but if i couldn't be with her forever
i'd settle for a little while

in truth
these words haunt me
ever since i wrote this
about a girl
who got away
i've been trying
desperately
to add to it
it always seemed incomplete
unfinished
but in a way
that's fitting
this piece will remain unfinished
just like her and i
always a thread to pull
but never pulled

the
ink stains
on my
hands
on my
arms
remind me
of the
stains
and bruises
you left
on my
body
heart
and soul

ninety-two. sailing, sailing.

i can't wait
for our first date
on a boat
per this note
a poetically priceless promise
of purposefully pretty proportions
we shall see
the open sea
sailing the world and more
adventure just outside our door

take my hand
as we stand
on the deck of our boat
per this note
a potentially poetic promise
of precisely pretentious proportions
the sun sets fast
this moment won't last
so hold my hand as we're sailing
sailing away

ninety-three. miles per hour.

ever find yourself in a moral dilemma
whether it was something big
or something insignificant
and no matter how hard you tried
you just couldn't bring yourself to decide
one way or the other
maybe it was because
there were emotions at stake
maybe it was because
there was money up for grabs
or maybe it was simply
pride fuckin' witchu
whatever it was
it just made your decision harder
and just when you thought it couldn't get any harder
she texts you
and she says she's horny
really horny
really horny and in need of your gentle touch
that was simply all you needed
to send you over the edge of indecisiveness
you dropped *everything*
and set a new record from camarillo to simi valley
twenty-three minutes to get from carmen avenue
to drop off one friend at erringer and fitzgerald
and another at lemon and alamo
only to find yourself waiting on scofield for nothing
and getting the text that you dreaded in the first place
"sleepy sorry goodnight"

for fucksake
you broke, like, at least five laws to get there in time
only to be met with an awful, yet surprisingly gentle

FUCK OFF

the universe doesn't take too kindly
to people who put sex before almost everything else

but hey
relax
it isn't *your* fault
not really
i mean
that's just the way life is
(right)

well that's the way life was for *me*
when i was young and dumb
which is to say
when i was *a fucking chauvinistic pile of dog shit*

i was one month away
from my fifth birthday
when the northridge earthquake hit
a solid 6.7
and even though
my memory is hazy
i recall
playing with my legos
all through the day before
i built magnificent castles
and wondrous spaceships
i had built so many, in fact
that they littered my bedroom floor
and the next morning
when everything shook
my door jamb shifted
forcing the door to my bedroom shut
i could hear my dad shouting
from the other side
telling me to
get under my bed
that he would come for me
so that's what i did
i got out of bed
i crawled underneath
i covered my ears
and closed my eyes
and i stayed silent
waiting for my dad to save me

it all happened so fast
but i remember
seeing my door burst open
and my dad fall to his knees near my bed
he landed right on top of all my legos
(he would later visit the hospital
and need stitches for those wounds)
he told me to crawl toward him
as pieces of the ceiling fell
and landed everywhere near him
some hit him
but he was unaffected
he grabbed my blanket
scooped me up
wrapped it around me
and all i saw was black for awhile
the next thing i remember
was being in the car
on the way to grandma's house
which wasn't far
the shaking stopped not long after
and there was some softer shaking later in the day
but it was over
and we were safe

the earthquake scarred me
the legos scarred him
and until the day he died
my dad carried those scars
and they always reminded me
that superheroes are real

ninety-five. windows.

i am fascinated by eyes
nuances of color and shape
i take great pleasure
in staring deeply into
the eyes of strangers
for one it's hilarious
the look on their faces
when you just stare at them
but i've also found
that aside from color
each eye has its own
snowflake pattern
with its own imperfections

these days
more often than not
people have trouble
looking others in the eye
some say
if someone isn't looking you in the eye
that they're being deceptive
but i've known some of the best liars
who could look you in the eye
and convince you of anything

but my favorite thing
by far
about eyes
is watching someone watch me talk

why
have you ever noticed
that sometimes
when you talk
peoples' eyes occasionally glance down
at your lips
an expert in body language
and facial expression
once told me
that watching someone's lips
while they talk
is a sign of attraction
that you're attracted to them
that you have a subconscious desire
to kiss them
and while that's always been
fascinating to think about
i've never really thought
it was true
i mean sure
it could be
i know i'm guilty
of staring at lips
especially kissable ones
but i also know
that sometimes
it's just fucking hard to hear people
over the stupid fucking conversations
other people are having at the bar
fucking trump supporters
i swear to me

ninety-six. irish lullaby.

warm
my heart
with
your soul
one
note
at
a
time
then
sing me
off to
sleep
and
i promise
i will
dream
of
you

ninety-seven. hollow.

when i
stand
alone
in an
empty
room
and i
hear the
screaming
silence
i smile
ever so
slightly
because
my brain
finally
understands
how my
heart feels

ninety-eight. degrees.

whenever life
gets you down
and i mean way down
way *way* down
kicks you to the curb
beats the *fuck* out of you
knocks you unconscious
and generally
gives you the
brock turner treatment
also sometimes referred to as
pulling a cosby
just remember
you are a fucking champion
you can make something of yourself
you are wonderful
and you **will** succeed
because
after all
if a band like
98 degrees
can make it big
with super creative and unique songs like
do you wanna dance
i wanna love you
and my personally favorite
heaven's missing an angel
then you can wake up for your morning classes
you fucking champion, you

ninety-nine. y2k.

does anybody remember
the great y2k scare
(if not, you're too young to be reading this)
how dumb were we
to assume that the machines *we* built
machines capable of taking us to the moon
and launching nuclear warheads with tactical precision
couldn't handle two zeros
it's almost as if
machines are only capable
of doing what we tell them to
and i'll tell you right now
if the y2k crash *had* gone down
i would hate to have been the guy who built the program
that couldn't handle two zeros

so the next time
something is troubling you
remember
an entire generation of adults
thought the world was going to end
because of zeros

one hundred. winchester.

you know
they say the whole
seeing someone from across the room thing
never happens in real life
but i can attest to the fact that
it totally does

i saw her
from across the room
okay
it was a bar
i saw her
from across the *bar*
we locked eyes
and in that moment
i knew
it was her
she was the one
this overwhelming sense of
joy
pure
joy
there was no convincing me otherwise
she was the one
(at least for that night)
i set my course
i steadied my sails
and off i went
there was no stopping me now
like a marathon runner

140

determined to finish
despite the chafing
as i approached
the moment drew near
i imagined us
her and i
together
intertwined
lost in a sea of
sheets and sex
her hair in my mouth
soft giggles
ow wrong hole
oops sorry
ooo right there
too hard
just right
faster
slower
make up your mind, woman
okay, okay
yes
yes
oh god yes
oh god no
ow ow ow
are you close
did you finish
okay but hurry up
not on my face
okay but don't get it in my hair

fuck
i said don't get any in my hair
sorry i have bad aim
fucking asshole
what
it was an accident
sure it was
whatever
no i don't want to cuddle
was it good for you
sure
could you fill out this survey card
what
please rate my overall performance
you're kidding right
your feedback will me help continue to provide excellent
service to future guests
get the fuck out
but
get out

well
that took the wind out of my sails

i didn't approach
not that night
it was for the best
because we would later become friends
and as it turns out
she's a lesbian
(with a girlfriend who is just as hot as she is)

142

there's a moral to this story
somewhere
fuck if i know what it is
but i *do* know
her and i are the best of friends
and at the end of the day
that's what *really* matters

oh
i will say
i do still fantasize
about a life with her
especially now that we're friends
which some people
might find weird
but i think it's endearing
because now that we've opened up to each other
i find that she's quite the remarkable person
and i definitely
need more remarkable people in my life

i'd be lying if i said
that i didn't often find myself thinking
"god i wish this girl was straight so we could date"
but
that's neither here nor there
what matters
is that we both love supernatural
she's the dean to my castiel
what more could i ask for
that's some ride or die shit right there

one hundred one. dalmatians.

i love living in socal
but it has its downsides
one of the things i hate
is the traffic
and one of the worst offenders
is the 101
but not for the reason you think
see
the 405, the 5, and the 10 are notorious
for basically being a parking lot
during rush hour
but the 101 has a different reputation
it's sort of like
a dalmatian
it's a super popular freeway
medium to large build
most people drive short, easy-to-drive distances on it
and it's generally a nice, enjoyable ride
but occasionally
whether it's because of road work
or an accident
or fuck it *just because*
it's fucking temperamental
and it's stop and go
stop and go
stop and *fucking go*
you'd think a fucking disney villain was behind it
plotting to take over the world
selling brake pads or some shit

one hundred two. shitty sequels and asshole cinephiles.

when did hollywood decide
that it was okay
to take great movies
and destroy them
with shitty sequels

look
i don't mean
to sound like every
dumb
sexist
overly opinionated
cinephile
on the internet
because *fuck them*
and their bullshit
but come on, hollywood
get your shit together

while we're on the subject
can i just say
fuck people who refer to themselves
as cinephiles
of course they'd call themselves something
pretentious *as fuck*
but aside from their bullshit self-chosen nickname
can we just talk about
how fucking full of shit they are
you know the type

they wear fedoras
or newsboy caps
they have some
grossly long beard
and not the cool viking kind either
the lame
"i shaved once and cut myself so now i'm afraid of razors"
kind
(at least that's what i assume they think
because they basically have neckbeards)
always thinking their opinion is the right one
they say things like
"everybody's entitled to their own opinion, *but…*"
or
"christopher nolan is a visionary"
they're the same people
that will praise marvel
for taking the time to really build a character like stark
but decry dc
for doing the same thing with batman
you know the kind
the kind that cum buckets
over everything joss whedon puts his fucking name on
the kind that waste their breath
trying to prove to you that
indiana jones would *totally* have died in that fridge
and that crystal skull is a terrible film because of it
come on now
that franchise has magical voodoo stones
face-melting god magic

and short round not getting punched in the face every time
he opens his little annoying fuckface mouth to gently
scream "dr. jones, dr. jones!"
and surviving a nuclear blast in a fridge is what gets you
no
just
no
shut the fuck up
just
shut the fuck up
seriously
you suck
and for the record
the force awakens was not *ruined*
because it had a female protagonist
and no
hollywood is not catering to women just because
rogue one also has a female protagonist
and even if they fucking were
would that be such a bad thing
hollywood has been "catering" to a male audience since
well
since *for-fucking-ever*
would it be so terrible
to see more empowered female protagonists

no
it wouldn't
you fucking pricks

fuck

one hundred three. empowered female protagonists.

speaking of
i'd like to take a moment
to acknowledge
an empowered female protagonist
in my life
her name is
well
her name isn't important
she knows who she is
but
who she is
is important
she is a powerful woman
but more importantly
a powerful *human*
who kicks ass
takes names
and chews bubblegum
(and she's all outta gum)
she deserves the world
but a poem will have to suffice
she inspires me to do great things
and i sure as hell
hate myself
whenever i let her down
so i strive
to do good
and i ask myself
w.w.k.d.

one hundred four. corinthian columns.

you have within you
the power to do good
but
you're human
so you might not always do so
and that's okay
your life isn't about
just doing good things
though that's what the religious folks will tell you
your life is yours
to do with as you see fit
so as long as you don't fuck up anyone else's life
i say
why not
why not embrace your humanity
you're human
nobody's going to fault you
for simply being human
well god might
if there is a god
he'd fault you for things you've never done
the bastard
i never understood
why god sees being human
and having human desires
and acting on them
as being such a terrible thing
personally i like zeus better
he gets me

one hundred five. to the exit on crenshaw.

growing up
i spent a fair amount of time
down in torrance
it was
well
not that fun
i have a few fond memories
like my mom taking us to jack in the box
and with the straightest face
ordering fifty tacos with no sauce
the person on the headset
always asked the same question
"did you say fifty tacos, or fifty sets of tacos"
bitch
i said fifty tacos
if i wanted one hundred tacos
i would have said one hundred tacos
that's what i thought to myself
but the best memories
weren't the silly ones
like my ex-stepdad kevin pretending to have tourettes
and shouting obscenities out the window
as we drove by elderly couples
or convincing my brother
to use a drumstick to scratch an itch in his asshole
no
the *best* memories
are the ones
where we're all together

like on holidays
sitting around the tree
or the dinner table
sharing stories
opening gifts
being a family together

it was always so hard
being a part of two different families
always feeling like
i was betraying one for the other
but looking back on it now
the truth is
i was incredibly lucky
some people
don't even have *one* family
and there i was
living among *two*
two sets of parents
relatives on both sides
love from both sides

i was never very good
at showing my appreciation
and now i'm at a point in my life
where i have very little family left
which
is probably the worst feeling in the world
i used to wish
i only had one family
now

i find myself wishing
i had any family at all

in recent days
i've tried to make peace with the family i do have
some are a part of my life
some aren't
but what's important
is appreciating them now
before i lose the chance
to show them i care
before i lose the opportunity
to tell them i love them
maybe you understand where i'm coming from
maybe you don't
maybe you've never had a family
or you've never had a traditional family
maybe you've had two families like me
whatever the case may be
i urge you to be a part of that
listen to their boring holiday stories
spend time with your boring cousins and their boring kids
be a part of the family
believe me when i say
you'll regret it if you don't

and if you don't have a family
remember that you have friends
and sometimes
friends are the only family you need

one hundred six. softly, swiftly, sincerely.

you
haven't left my
mind
still thinking
there could be
an us
(looks like anus)
but
there isn't
at least
not now
there can't be
too bad
i can
see it now
(i can always see it now)
in bed
with netflix
and blankets
and tea
blissful
i know
but oh well
for now
i'll just
sit here
alone
'til then
softly, swiftly, sincerely
wasting away

one hundred seven. a sincere apology, overdue.

dear mary-anne steelcrowe
(this is a character she played in a musical
i'm sure she'd hate if i used her real name)
our time together was
well
quite frankly
fucked
and since this is an apology
and i'm being honest
it was all my fault
(okay, *mostly* my fault)
ours was a rocky relationship
putting it mildly
putting it *bluntly*
i was a fucking asshole
and you were a crazy bitch
it had its moments
we had *our* moments
i have more than a few fond memories
from our time together
some are even positive
but *truly*
the faults in the relationship
stem from my inability to communicate
but before we get into this
i just want to say
that none of the following will excuse what i did
i simply want you and everyone else to understand
why i did what i did

154

see
the thing is
i didn't *want* a relationship
i was fresh out of one
i was living the single life
that many people dream of living
I can't help but be jealous of my past self
but then
you came along
and turned my world upside down
(you were great at that)
I struggled
with my feelings for you
and my desire to remain single
out of fear
of being hurt
of screwing up another relationship
as bad as I screwed up my last few
and at times
it was simply overwhelming
I couldn't stand *not* being with you
but being in a relationship was suffocating
I wanted you
but I didn't want the pressure
I wanted love
without the responsibility
not because I have a fear of commitment itself
but because I fear losing that commitment
i'm constantly stressing myself out
over pleasing my partner
making sure my partner is happy

that I neglect myself
my anxiety level rises
and I break
and run away and hide
in an attempt to ease my anxiety
and put myself back together
that's what you walked into
when you came into my life
a horrid mess
barely able to put *myself* together
and that mess
fell in love with you
my fear of failing
my fear of losing you
is what ultimately caused me
to lose you

we fought
a lot
and that's still an understatement
those who were closest to us
definitely know
we fought more than i've ever fought
with any woman
in all my relationships put together
and that's *still* an understatement
we fought about trivial things
things so trivial
that even acknowledging we fought about them
seems trivial
we fought

but somehow
we made it work for a long time
we stuck by each other through a lot
you were here for me when no one else was
and i for you
(even if you choose to ignore that fact)
we were two peas
and life was our oyster
what went wrong
(so many things)

i struggled with my feelings
while we were together
back and forth
back and forth
first we were lovers
then we were best friends
then lovers again
and for a while we were even both
(that was the best)
but somewhere along the line
something changed
i woke up one morning
and everything was different
i couldn't say when
or what
or why
but things were different
drastically different
and there was no going back
no matter how hard we both tried

i do want to say
that there was a period of time
where you
flat out supported me
you paid the rent
you fed the cat
you fed *me*
and in retrospect
it probably felt like
i wasn't contributing
and that's partially true
but what i never told you
was that most of my money
went into a savings account
that i had created
to help me save up
to buy you a ring
which i'm sure sounds like bullshit
even to everyone else reading this
but that's the truth
no sense lying about it now
it's not like that redeems me
or makes me look like less of an asshole
nope
still the same asshole
guilty of the same horrible shit
but even so
it was a ring
a sign of my love
that you never got
(add it to the list)

now i know what you're thinking
you're thinking
"you cheated on me
that's why we broke up
you fuck"
which is true
yes
it's true
all this time
i've been trying to forget
to convince myself
that it wasn't true
but it is
i met someone
(someone who would later become my ex-wife
karma's a bitch and certainly has a sense of humor)
and i fell for her
we never kissed
not while you and i were still together
but that doesn't matter
emotional cheating is still cheating
and that was that
that was the end
and
i've still never forgiven myself
and probably never will
which
again
doesn't mean much
but it is what it is

a few days before we split
we met in the parking lot
of the fancy target near my place
we sat in your car
we talked for hours
i could feel your anger
your sorrow
your eagerness to hold on
you could feel my distance
my coldness
my desire for someone else
but you didn't say anything
and we talked
and we fought
and we talked some more
and the night ended
with a promise to try
to try harder
to make things work
to stick together *no matter what*
but all the while
i kept trying to bring myself
to end things
i was afraid
because despite what you believe
i loved you
i loved you with all my heart
i didn't want to hurt you
looking back
i realize now that i was being selfish
it's true though

i did love you
(and i still do)
i didn't want to hurt you
(and i still don't)
but i also
didn't want to hurt myself
and i knew losing you
would hurt the most

look
you probably think i'm full of shit
and most of the time i am
but when it comes to this
it's from the heart
(not that you believe that either)
i loved you
i just wasn't *in* love with you
(they call them clichés for a reason)
and from experience
having that realization
is one of *the* worst feelings in the world
but what's even *worse*
is still loving someone
who will never love you back
you've moved on now
your life is much better without me in it
and i'm happy for you
no jokes
or snide remarks
just happiness
i'm happy that you're happy

one hundred eight. with an h, like hate.

take it from me
one of the worst feelings in the world
is coming between two friends
and being the reason they aren't friends anymore
and one of the worst ways to do that
is by falling for someone
and then falling for their best friend
tricky business, that is

i didn't mean to
you can't help who you like
though i suppose
one could do a better job
at keeping those feelings to oneself

in college
i did a lot of theater
and one semester
while casting a show
i met two girls
mary-anne steelcrowe
(the girl from one hundred seven)
and
thought-she-was-a-christian girl
(what can i say, i'm terrible at names)
and instantly
i fell madly for
thought-she-was-a-christian girl
what a twist

but as time passed
and we worked together
and hung out
i thought
there is no way in hell
this girl would ever like me
and that was that

fast forward a few months
and mary-anne steelcrowe and i
got involved
(see one hundred seven)
and during our
on again
off again
whatever-you-want-to-call-it relationship
i found that
my feelings for
thought-she-was-a-christian girl
wouldn't go away
they were just *there*
haunting me
we would all hang out
and my thoughts would drift
to her and i

and then one day
when i couldn't bear the thought
of going another day
keeping these feelings to myself
i told her

i called her
and confessed
fully expecting
she would laugh it off
and that would be that
but
that's not what happened
no
i called her
and confessed

"really"
followed by silence
yes, really
why would i say it
if it wasn't true
"okay, so, i feel the exact same way"

what?
"i've had a crush on you since we met
but like
megan brought up having a crush on you
and you seemed to like her too
so i just
kept it to myself"

fuck
fuck
fuckfuckfuckfuckfuck

are you kidding me
you mean to tell me
this whole time
this whole fucking time
that i've been pining for you
that i've casually and innocently flirted with you
and daydreamed we could be together
we could have
actually been together
fuck
"so what are we going to do about this"
right there
right *fucking* there
i should have said
"things are the way they are
i'm with mary-anne steelcrowe now
you two are best friends
nothing can ever come of this
even if her and i broke up
because
you two are best friends
and i don't ever want to come between you two"
that's what i should have said

obviously things got messy
and things ended poorly
they are no longer friends
and both of them hate me now
but the moral of the story is
always follow your heart
and never your libido

one hundred nine. speechless.

your eyes
they flirt
with mine
our souls
they dance
intertwined
your heart
it speaks
to mine
inviting me
to be
with you

that look
you know the one
that look
only you can give
that look
that says
so many things at once
that look
i'm speechless
which is slightly humorous
being a writer
i'm speechless
that look
you know the one

one hundred ten. it's cold and it's grey.

it's cold and it's grey
the perfect pair
wouldn't you agree
clouds in the sky
overshadow us
the cold and the grey
goosebumps
up and down
that feeling
when i close my eyes
imagining you're here
with me
in this weather
the cold and the grey
you'll come back
someday
but until then
i'll be here
in this weather
the cold and the grey
close your eyes now
think of me
i'll think of you
it's cold and it's grey
the perfect pair
wouldn't you agree

one hundred eleven. oh goudie.

you bitch
how could you

that was harsh
let me start again

you bitch
oh i hate when that happens
you think back
on the good times
with someone
but your memories
are spoiled
by that one thing

we had a thing
i don't know if it was a *good* thing
or a *terrible* thing
but it was *our* thing
sex at the office
bruises and bite marks
rug burns and handprints
it was a *sexy* thing
if nothing else
but we said
we said no catching feelings
and then i caught feelings
so i guess it's my fault after all
(when is it not)

but i tried
my very best
and somehow
it wasn't good enough
i hate when that happens
don't you
you bitch
there it goes again

you broke up with me at work
at work
you did it so i couldn't say anything
couldn't argue
couldn't fight for us
you wanted a quick way out
you thought it'd be painless
you were wrong

you don't owe me anything
do whatever you want
you do you, boo
in some ways
you were right to walk away
and it's okay
for us to both admit it

you've moved on now
and that's great
you deserve to be happy
you bitch

okay
let's clear the air
every single time
this topic comes up
with a girl
she thinks
i'm trying to convince her
to send me nudes
look
i love nudes
i'm almost certain
that's what snapchat is truly for
but just because
i mention how much
i love random nudes
throughout the day
or late at night
whenever
that doesn't mean
i'm trying to *convince* you to send them
sending nudes isn't for everyone

but for the record
i *never* screenshot
without permission

(okay, valid point
but in my defense
tits are awesome)

pretty sure
i'm not helping my case
what i mean is
nudes are great
nudes are great when they come from a place
of self confidence
nudes born of
sexual desire
or peer pressure
those nudes *suck ass*
but confidence nudes
nudes that showcase
a confident person
displaying their body
with pride
those are bomb fuckin' nudes
we need more of that
more self confidence
more pride
we need that shit on display
so we can show future generations
what it means to be confident
to take pride in yourself
in who you are
in what you have

fuck
i bet that's the deepest
anyone has ever gotten
about nudes
real talk

one hundred thirteen. trekkie.

you know
one of the truly frustrating things
about the world we live in
is that there is some
implied hierarchy
even between
people of the same age and class
for example
this girl i know
we'll call her
trekkie
she's my former boss
we're about the same age
but when we met
(when she hired me)
there was this implied hierarchy between us
she was the boss
i was the employee
and that's how it was
even though
the more we worked together
the more we realized
we were pretty much friends
minus the whole hanging out outside of work thing
but i always felt like
she felt the need to keep it professional
which was *super* disappointing
because i always felt like
we would make *really* good friends

and of course
if you hadn't guessed by now
i was always super attracted to her
i mean
you can't really blame me
we were both
covered in tattoos
we had dozens of common interests
we were both super sarcastic
and both outspoken feminists
honestly
i'm surprised it never came up
though
if she hadn't moved back to boston
i'm almost certain it would have
eventually
(maybe that's wishful thinking on my part)

but where most people
saw a fiery redhead
i saw a strong
dedicated
hard working woman
making a name for herself
in a world that looks down on women
sees them as second class citizens
where most people
saw a bitchy hardass of a boss
i saw a woman
talked down to by her male peers
told she didn't know as much as men

most people
when they hear me talking
about being attracted to a woman
they just assume
that i'm talking about
physical attraction
now
i'm not saying
that I *don't* give off that vibe
i totally get why people think that
i guess in some ways
i fit the stereotypical
cisgenerded straight male
but
the truth is
i am attracted to her
as a person
everything about her
how she carries herself
how she speaks
everything about her is
in a word
strong
she's educated
she's dedicated
she's authentic
and you just don't find that in people anymore

so yeah
i hoped we had the chance
to be something more

she's a catch
worth cherishing
and even though
i may never
be the one
to cherish her
to admire her
or honor her
in that way
i can only hope
that she finds *someone*
that thinks as highly of her
as i do
because
if she does
then she'll be a lucky girl

but
it's also worth noting
that even if she *doesn't*
she always has herself
and that's just as great
(if not better)

and sticking with this twilight zone thing
if you're reading this, trekkie
if we ever do have the chance
it would be an honor
to partner with you
and stand beside
someone as fantastic as you

all i want in this life
is to have a partner
who looks at me
the way
sam looked at frodo
at the end of
return of the king
sam and frodo
that's the epitome of
ride or die
sam carried frodo
when he couldn't walk
literally carried him
frodo is a lucky hobbit
if i find a partner
who is half as loyal
as samwise is to frodo
fuck
i'd give up sex for that
if only i could be so lucky
here's hoping

get yourself a partner
who will carry your ass
through a fucking volcano
but who will also
post embarrassing photos of the whole thing
and ridicule you endlessly for being a little *bitch*
ride or die motherfucker

176

one hundred fifteen. plaid skirts and pushup bras.

hello
a warm welcome
an offer of friendship
however brief
with a smile
and a beer
we're friends

you're beautiful
i'm not
to me
you're unobtainable
to you
i'm a dollar sign
because that's what this is
a friendship
based on money
based on a service
and that service
is selling me your beer
and yourself
if only for the night
(and me footing the bill)

you're lovely
and i'm wealthy
and that's what really matters
isn't it
i'm a dollar sign

but that's okay
because
it's worth it
you're worth it
for the night anyway
i think you are
that plaid skirt
your ass hanging out
just enough
to entice
your pushup bra
a master display
it distracts me
from the truth
of our friendship
you're a service
and i'm a dollar sign

but just for a moment
let's pretend
it's more than that
let's pretend
we're more
we're more than our commodity
let's pretend
we're humans
and that
even for a brief moment
there's a real connection between us

hello

one hundred sixteen. slap bet.

it started with a bet
a stupid bet
i was sure to win
but yet
you won
on a technicality
but still
a win nonetheless
i didn't think you'd do it
slap me
but yet
you did
it wasn't very hard
but still
it stung
but the loss
stung more
despite the loss
i was excited
when you slapped me
i thought
if there wasn't a spark before
you sure as hell made one

it started with a bet
a stupid bet
and if i'm being honest
i'm glad i didn't win
(though i'm still waiting for that spark)

one hundred seventeen. fingering Am.

don't let the title fool you
this is going to get real
real fast
see the thing is
i have many apologies to make
for many terrible things
most of them too long or too serious
to be written here
but what i can apologize for
is my shitty chauvinist behavior
(which is why
so many of these
apologies
are to women)
speaking of
there was a girl
we'll call her
Am *(like the musical note)*
and i'll just go ahead and say
she was seventeen
and i was twenty-three
we dated for two or three months
it was actually pretty great
she was an old soul
even more mature than me at times
honestly
it was one of the best
definitely the one of the healthiest
relationships i've ever had

things were absolutely great
so obviously
i needed to find a way
to fuck it up

her birthday was coming up
everyone was excited
i was too
she was turning eighteen
but before you get all pervy
that's not the reason why i was excited
she made it clear
she was waiting for the right guy
and i made it clear
that i wasn't interested in sex
we were together because
we were both intellectuals
we were both talented artists
and we enjoyed our time together
i was excited because
i was going to meet more of her family
and all of her close friends from back home
i was excited to be a part of her family
but then
a week before her birthday
we were out together
and out of nowhere
i broke her heart
she told me she was falling in love with me
it was the best moment i had had
in a long time

and then
just as i was on cloud nine
i said the dumbest thing
i could have fucking said
"i feel the same
but there's a part of me
that will always love someone else"
which is true
but not in a romantic way
i will always love this girl from college
whose name is not relevant to this apology
but
that didn't mean i *wasn't* in love with Am
no
i *was* in love with Am
(i am *in love with Am)*
she asked me what i meant
and i lied
"there's just this
other side of me
sort of like
another personality
his name is heathcliff"
and that did it
because she knew what i meant
heathcliff is the name
of a character from a play i wrote
(drop dead chauvinist)
and in that play
heathcliff is in love with his roommate
a woman named laura

182

and with that
she knew
and it broke her heart
i broke her heart
she sat there
and she cried
and there was nothing i could do
but watch
as the one thing i wanted
more than anything in this world
was heartbroken
because of me
i watched her slip away
right before my eyes
i watched as she began
to fall out of love with me
and honestly
it was one of the most painful things
i've ever watched

to this day
the thing i regret the most
was breaking her heart
she'll *never* forgive me
and that's okay
because i'll never forgive myself

one hundred eighteen. simi valley.

say what you will
about suburban living
but i sleep like a
fucking baby

it may be offensive to some
but i enjoy my privilege
my white male straight cisgendered privilege
i have not a care in the world
except maybe
how much data i use on my cell phone
or whether or not
naked juice is on sale this month
the thing is though
i acknowledge my privilege
it's a real thing
and i absolutely use my privilege
to act out against gender and racial inequality
it may not be much
but it's better than simply
basking in my privilege
from my middle class apartment
with my middle class sedan
posting about it
on the latest iphone

what have *you* done
to help abolish gender and racial inquality
lately

one hundred nineteen. red leather jacket.

soft, painful pressure
intensifies
as the grip your teeth have
on my skin
tightens
i can feel my heartbeat
the blood coursing through my veins
it's pumping faster
to help me satisfy my urge
to take you
my hand
slides down your back
our nails digging into each other's skin
my teeth grip your skin now
my right hand
finds your lower back
as i pull your body closer
and closer
while my left hand
finds your neck
and for a brief moment
you can't breathe
and your pleasure intensifies
as i bring you closer
and closer
to the edge
and the rest
as they say
is up to your imagination, darling

one hundred twenty. dorkasaurus rex.

everyone needs a
dorkasaurus rex
in their life
someone unafraid
to dance like nobody's watching
when everyone is watching
someone unhindered
by societal norms
who dances to their own tune
i have a dorkasaurus rex
in my life
and i'm grateful
awkward turtles
third grade talent show dance moves
and rapping the sweet ghetto sounds
of the great dr dre
truly
an unabashed
uninhibited
and unapologetic
free spirit
a nerd
a geek
and everything in between
a true
dorkasaurus rex
my love for her
is beyond romantic
true love, *truly*

one hundred twenty-one. piano concerto no.23.

tear drops
they drip from her eyelids
slowly they fall down
the sides of her miserable
beautiful face
down and across her
blood-colored lips
i imagine they'd be salty
as the music plays
she dances
as do her tears
she glides across the room
gracefully
with the stained blue silk from her dress
dragging softly behind her
teardrops
and mascara
those stains
that's what they are
i am her partner
and i cannot take my eyes off of her
i see her tears
as they streak
her makeup is running
her skin losing color
as her legs give out
and she falls
to the ground
i catch her

my right hand
braces her miserable
beautiful face
my left catches her back
a single tear
struggles to make its way
to my fingertips
my fingertips
and through my own tears
i manage a smile
faint
but still
through her tears
and the pain
and her ruined makeup
through her suffering
and her sadness
i see her smile
her last breath
finally escapes her tortured
blood-colored lips
and all i can think about
are the tears
on my fingertips
my fingertips
i raise them to my lips
and as i did
through all of the misery
i could see the sunrise through the window
and at last
a new day had come

one hundred twenty-two. naudy.

i asked you once
why we're still friends
and you told me
it's because
i'm a good person at heart
i think you're wrong
i'm sure
there are plenty of people
who would disagree with you
but that doesn't stop you
you're still here
we're still friends
don't get me wrong
i am *more* than grateful
but it makes me wonder

i asked you once
why you're still here
and you told me
we're friends
and friends don't leave
and i'm grateful
because i don't have
many of those
people who stay
no matter what
that's what friends do

you're a true friend

and as a true friend
you deserve
much more love
and appreciation
than i've *ever* given you
you put up with me
and that's more
than most people will do
you put up with me
and my bullshit
you're a fucking saint
do you know that
i'm sure you do

despite how many times
i've said this to you
i'm sorry
i truly am
you came into my life
at the worst possible time
that isn't *your* fault
that's just how things were
i fucked us up
you deserved better
you deserve better
than i could *ever* give you
but you're still here
that's love
even if you won't call it that
(but don't worry
your secret's safe with me)

one hundred twenty-three. kiki.

our eyes met
across a crowded bar
a twenty-first century
love story
and that's
where it ended
even before
it began
it was all in my head
our twenty-first century
romance
we'd sing karaoke
then buy each other drinks
our connection
as strong as airport wifi
snapchat this
instagram that
tweeting and texting
and sharing
and blogging
our life together
a twenty-first century
love affair
can you see it now
or should i
reblog the link again
one new notification
your chat session has ended
user is no longer online

one hundred twenty-four. platinum smile.

have you ever given a thought to
the strangeness of
the relationships you have
with strangers
like
the girl who works at in'n'out
i see her almost every time i'm there
we both smile
ask each other how things are going
swap entertaining stories
i order my protein style burger
and then life goes on
but in all this time
that we've shared this time together
i've never stopped to think
just how odd this must look
say
to people from small towns who know everyone
i see this girl *so often*
we know so much about each other
where we work
which classes she's failing
which customers i hate working with
where we went on our last respective vacations
but yet
i don't know her last name
i know *so much* about her
that i'm just now realizing
i know *so little* about her

which
honestly
makes me think
about the people i call friends
the fact that we can go through life
sharing so many experiences
but knowing *so little* about each other
it's kind of sad when you think about it
people can spend their whole lives
around other people
making friends
swapping stories
laughing together
but still somehow
know *nothing* of substance about one another
but as for *this* girl
she remains a mystery
there's this feeling of mystery
and you know i love *my mystery*
but beyond that
i almost feel as if
there's this unreasonably high expectation
like she has this image of me
has given me some backstory
(which a lot of people in retail and food service do)
and she doesn't want to find out
i'm way less interesting in real life
or maybe i think that about her
or maybe
i'm making excuses
and i'm just too chicken to ask her out

one hundred twenty-five. my blue-haired addiction.

periodically in life
you'll meet a soul
who you feel
closely matches your own
a kindred spirit
someone who feels
like a missing piece of you
or someone whose soul
has this strange magnetism toward yours
these people we sometimes meet
are hard to stay away from
but sometimes
impossible to be near
that's what she was to me
someone i couldn't stay away from
but couldn't bring myself to stay with
there was a soft kindness about her
it was inviting
enticing
infectious
i couldn't turn away
and then eventually
some wasn't enough
i needed her
her touch
her smile
her kiss
but these were all things
in short supply

not for me
demand
but no supply
and that was okay
with my *brain*
but my *heart*
was a different story
i distanced myself
because i was afraid
afraid of how my soul would feel
if i got *too close*
and then suddenly lost her
so i shut down
pulled away
and that was that

there are times where
i regret
walking away
but when those times hit
and trust me
they hit *hard*
i force myself
to think back
and remember
my addiction
she was
my addiction

i may be sober
but i'll never be clean

one hundred twenty-six. favorite.

you're it
thought i couldn't say
what *it* is
little things
like the way you speak
little things
like the way you smell
little things
like how you don't just put up with me
but you enjoy being around me
that or
you're the best actor in the world
it's one thing
when you're co-workers
to *have* to be around someone
it's another thing entirely
to make the most
out of all your time together
and that's what we do
we joked
that we'll pretend that there's
sexual chemistry between us
you joked
i was delirious
i joked
that you were in denial
but we both know
that there's *something* there
(i'm sure your fiancé wont' mind)

one hundred twenty-seven. hours.

i've always been fascinated
by the passage of time
or to be more specific
our perception of the passage of time
we all know that time
only moves in one direction
and it's safe to say
that we all agree
that the concept of time
time as we measure it with clocks
is a human construct
that time has the value that we assign it
which in our society
is a *huge* value
but what i'm *more* concerned with
is *our* perception of time and its passage
everyone has experienced
time seemingly moving fast and slow
that's where the expression
time flies
comes from
everyone has had one of those days
at school or at work
where you've been having so much fun
or you've been working so hard
that time seems to slip away
one moment you're talking and having fun
and before you know it
it's the end of the day

but everyone has also experienced
time moving like *a fucking snail*
it's boring
there's nothing to do
but sit and stare at the clock
and time seems to slow down
as if
you staring at the clock
makes it *want* to slow down
just to piss you off
(time is a dick like that)
but what most people *don't* know
is that this effect
is actually based on science
see
the brain has a lot of information to process
and it doesn't need dead air shoved in there
so instead
it starts to condense the dead air
and you perceive it as less time passing
now
when this happens
it's not like your brain is manipulating time
or time traveling
it's more like
when you open a program on your computer
then look away
and when you look back
the program is open
to you
that program opened as soon as you clicked it

you didn't perceive the program loading
but you *know* it did
your brain does the same sort of thing
but instead of looking away
it simply filters what it processes
(cool trick, though i wish it would filter trips to the dmv)
there are also some cool theories
as to other reasons why
our perception of time changes
the amount of time that passes is relative to one's age
think about that
to a five year old
one year is one fifth of their entire life
but to a fifty year old
one year is *two percent* of their entire life
so the value of time is significantly different
and then there's the idea
that our internal clock
our biological clock, if you will
begins to slow with age
we call that *getting fucking old*
but as we age
and our bodily processes begin to slow down
it appears as though time is passing more quickly
relative to us moving more slowly
and *then*
there's this idea
that as kids
we pay more attention to time
think about christmas
we stay up late waiting for santa

we count down the days
but as we get older
and certain things come to light
(i won't say it because i'm not a fucking savage)
we're naturally less excited
things seem more inevitable
we see less need to count down
because we expect they'll happen regardless
and we're more focused on accomplishing tasks
like paying bills
meeting deadlines for work
you know
boring adult stuff
so with less emphasis
on anticipation
and more emphasis
on efficiency
we begin to eschew the build up
and cut to the chase
(another well-known expression)
and *of course*
there's the idea
that as kids
we measure the passage of time
with *firsts*
first kiss
first car
first fight
and as we get older
we experiences fewer firsts
because we're becoming more experienced

so
all of that being said
to say this:
time is valuable
you only get so much of it
and
even the time we *do* get
is subject to change
upon perception
so
maybe
try keeping things in perspective
one year may be
three or four percent of your life
but that doesn't change
its importance
you may be getting older
but that doesn't mean
you should be less excited
for things you enjoy
you may be running out of firsts
but that just means
it's time to start expanding your horizon
because
as my dad used to say
"There's no substitute for experience."
and there will always be things
to experience
you just have to be willing
to find the time
so try setting a fucking alarm

one hundred twenty-eight. for the love of Bukowski.

there's this girl
a girl from tennessee
we'll call her
the girl from tennessee
just kidding
we'll call her
bukowski
we met on tumblr
she reminds me of
wednesday addams
sans the dress
and there's this
connection
this
strange chemistry
between us
(for me anyway)
i can't quite place it
it's odd
in a good way
but it reminds me
that sometimes
my hopeless romanticism
gets a bit carried away
because
she's wonderful
and i find myself
periodically
checking my phone

to see if she's texted
or send me a snapchat
because
there's something about her
that i can't explain
something about
the way we are
when we talk
that gives me
butterflies

oh for the love of
bukowski
because god's got nothing to do with it

but beyond all that
beyond bukowski
and these feelings
it makes me think
before the internet
before the advancement
of long distance communication
it would have been *impossible*
to easily meet people
outside of my own little
socal bubble
like people from different states
like bukowski
so even though i may be *crazy*
the way we met
makes me appreciate her

and our friendship
that much more
we're friends because
the internet is a thing
and when people say
technology is separating us
my only thought
is of
bukowski

technology is better than ever
and it allows us to connect
with people around the world
and it has allowed me
to connect with a girl
a girl from tennessee
bukowski
and dream a little dream
of a life
with her
full of dive bars
late night dumpster dives
and stevie nicks vibes

one hundred twenty-nine. opirum.

"there seems
to me
to always
be
a stigma upon opium
passed down from mum to mum
in fact
i see
opium
for me
is best when mixed with rum"

-samuel taylor coleridge (probably)

one hundred thirty. the person from porlock.

departing from porlock
determined to walk
he traveled fast with intent
for the reason he was sent
was to conduct his business with sam coleridge
at quite an early hour
so through the city and across the bridge
he walked to coleridge's tower

upon arrival, the discov'ry grim
poor coleridge topped up to the brim
the person from porlock did find him
strung out on equal parts opium
dissolved within coleridge's rum
as ol' sammy was scribbling away
about what the porlockian could not say

their business would soon be concluded
but it seemed sammy's brain had just farted
for poor coleridge's brain was eluded
by the reason his 'lock friend departed

for years they have wondered
every poem they've plundered
but still they know not who had come
who walked all that way
from porlock that day
and saw sam strung out on opirum

one hundred thirty-one. cruelty.

never date a writer
they're cruel
without asking
they take part of your soul
and make it their own
it becomes theirs to do with
as they will
they shape it
bend it to their will
they love it
they hate it
they fuck it
they kill it
that part of your soul
is theirs now
you'll be immortal
living on
long after you die
in the heart of a writer
your soul
gracing their pages
never date a writer
they're cruel
and if you ever break up
you can be sure
they've tortured themselves over you
never date a writer
they're cruel to themselves
over you

one hundred thirty-two. summers love.

a kiss
a simple kiss
that's all it took
you were drunk
i don't know
you kissed me
and it was done
you kissed me
and it was fun
you kissed me
called me hun
not your type
that's all i think
not your type
unless you drink
that's okay
you're too hot
that's okay
because i'm not
that's okay
a crazy thought
don't mind me
thinking out loud
no big deal really
just a thought
i've entertained
way too long
that's okay
friends it is

one hundred thirty-three. love's entire.

and now i've come to see where beauty lies
this happiness has found its way to me
your gentle smile and wondrous crystal eyes
bring forth these endless joys in jubilee
what sense it makes to kiss your luscious lips
and find myself adrift deep in your soul
a thousand things i'd give to trace your hips
with fingertips across your body whole
though days and nights pass i can't satisfy
my hunger for your beauty on my tongue
i've learned that lust serves just to pacify
but love will sate and keep you feeling young
we may still lust for romance and desire
but now we long for love in its entire

one hundred thirty-four. lookalike.

it starts
with a look
it almost always does
you looked
like her
i couldn't
help
but
fall
i felt bad
you could tell
which
made me feel
even worse
i fell
because of her
but
i stayed
because of you

one hundred thirty-five. othello.

i laughed
when i heard you directed othello
i laughed because
in an abstract way
i'm roderigo
and you're desdemona
if only in the sense that
for all my efforts to win your heart
i'll probably end up
in some dark place
between actual friendship
and forever pining
after doing some desperate thing
to win your affection
(sans the murdery bit)
but then i heard you also *played* othello
and that made even more sense
because
in an abstract way
you're othello
and i'm desdemona
if only in the sense that
i am completely devout
and my feelings for you are genuine
but all i imagine you see
is someone desperate for attention
maybe it's better this way
i'd hate to find out
that one of us is iago

one hundred thirty-six. on the importance of family.

sometimes
you don't realize
how important family is
until you don't have one

i lost my family once
it didn't happen overnight
it was a process
one that i let happen
i could have stopped it
but i was too concerned
with my own life
that i had no regard
for the lives of those around me

i had a brother once
a half-brother
who used to share his playstation with me
who used to come to me for advice
we were close
but not anymore
now there's nothing but
resentment
for the things i've said and done
for the things i never said or did
there's anger
and there's hatred
where there should be
love and affection

but i'll never get that brother back
even if we reconcile
those were innocent times
young and dumb
full of hope and love and
plans to change the world together
that's gone
why
because i was too busy
feeling sorry for myself
being a tortured soul
and condemning myself
to this unfulfilled life
i had a brother once
a brother
who i loved
and who loved me

i have two younger sisters
half-sisters
two teenage half-sisters
who miss their eldest brother
they miss playing dress up
and painting together
they miss mini-golf
and amusement parks
and making fun of the time
i convinced my brother to
scratch an itch inside his asshole
with a drumstick
we were close

but not anymore
and now there's nothing but
longing
for the brother they used to have
for the brother i used to be
there's sorrow
and there's emptiness
where there should be
joy and happiness
one day they'll get that brother back
it just takes time
time for me to dedicate myself
to the brother they deserve
because they're young
not quite innocent
but they need their older brother
why
because
this world is harsh and unkind
and even though
they can take care of themselves
they deserve someone
who will love them unconditionally
and guide them through this fucked up world
i have two younger sisters
two teenage sister
who deserve their eldest brother

i found my older sister
half-sister
a sister i never knew i had

and she needs family
family that understands
family that embraces
i need that family too
but i've had that family
i neglected that family
but now
now is the time to fix that
to be the brother i was
so long ago
not just to my siblings
i've had in my life
but also to the sister i have now
the sister that deserves the world
all the love and affection
all the joy and happiness
the world has to offer
all that i have to offer
she's never had a brother
she's never been disappointed by a brother
but now
she has me
and i have her
we both deserve each other
why
because
we're family
that's why

one hundred thirty-seven. angry beavers.

she's lovely
she's all the things men want
and then some
more though
at least to me
that's what makes her
her
laughter
in no short supply
different
but the same
a light in life
never dim
that's her
always out of reach
but worth trying
don't hold back
not now
it's funny
she's tough
no nonsense
but
more like daggett than norbert
see
funny how that works
(irrelevant but
because you're thinking it
i'll go ahead and say it
street sweeeeeeeeeeper)

one hundred thirty-eight. dungeons and dragons.

a lot of people criticize me
for playing dungeons and dragons
so i felt the need to say something
go fuck yourself
d&d is a great game
i hate to be cliché
but you people who knock it
really need to try
it allows us to tell a story
in a non-conventional method
stories full of
romance
suspense
danger
excitement
heroics
how is that lame
(it's not)
plus the best part
you get to play it with *friends*
i never fucking understood
why d&d was seen as
anti-social
you need friends to play d&d
d&d is like playing a video game
but *you* control the characters *and* the story
and you can drink beer with your friends while you do it
good luck finding people
who are willing to watch *you* drink and play skyrim

to this day
i've built
one hundred thirty-eight characters
(no, i haven't played them all)
i've created entire worlds
drawn players in with
mystery and intrigue
watched players
and characters
grow and mature
some over the course of years
literal years
we've tackled some taboo subjects
dealt with current issues
i've helped players with social issues
break out of their bubbles
i've helped players with mental illness
cope with their lives
d&d isn't just a game
it's an experience
it can be a whole other life for some
an escape from the real world
the chance to be a hero
to explore and develop a sense of morality
it's an avenue for self-expression
it's a living art form
and a cool one at that
i mean
dragons
come on

one hundred thirty-nine. black beauty.

i've owned
quite a few cars
in my day
but none as
treasured
as the
black beauty
christine
she was a buick
a slick eighties buick
pearlescent black
chrome rims
dashboard hula girl
big fuzzy dice
she had it all
lotta good memories
in that car
and it always reminds me
of when life was
easier
also known as
when life didn't suck so fucking much
people were alive
things we're positive
and it always seemed like
the sun shined a little brighter
things change
cars get old
but the memories never will

one hundred forty. lowe and behold.

my life is full of fantasy
dreaming of a girl to be
with for the rest of my days
a girl to change my evil ways
but lowe and behold
this beauty untold
a girl who i crave
to kiss and misbehave
with in the back seat
of my car to raise the heat
and heighten pleasure
to unmeasureable levels
like the devils down below
who torture sinners just for show
and love the sound of constant screaming
as the tension in the room
begins to rise as pleasure blooms
between this girl i long to kiss
despite my failings i persist
to pull her near
and grab her rear
as she slaps my face again
it's getting harder to pretend
that there is something here between us
though the tension can't be seen thus
the illusion there is hope for me
despite the fact i'll never be
a man that glitters gold
lowe and behold

one hundred forty-one. hot friend.

is there some
unwritten rule
somewhere
some
cosmic fucking imperative
that states
hot people
have
hot friends
do attractive people
seek out other
attractive people
and form some sort of
attraction
(see what i did there)
and congregate near
unattractive people
simply to
show off
i guess i'll never know
but
speaking of hot friends
lowe and behold
a beautiful person
friends with
a beautiful person
and
predictably
i can't keep my eyes off either of them

but
as usual
i find myself
writing about her
instead of
talking to her
because
i'm nothing
if not consistent
besides
writing about it
means i get to
imagine
things going
however i want them to
and believe me
when i say
things *always* go better
when i write about them

you're a
beautiful person
inside and out
and i
i am not
i am ugly
on the inside
but maybe one day
i'll fix myself
and
you'll finally see me

eyes
like
christmas lights
hair
like
tinsel
smile
like
nutcrackers
laugh
like
greensleeves
smell
like
gingerbread
body
like
sugar plum fairies
voice
like
carolers
nose
like
rudolph
love
like
christmas

one hundred forty-three. knockin' on heaven's door.

on the outside
looking in
knocking like a
girl scout hustler
begging for the chance
i've even got thin mints and tagalongs
(fuck samoas)

i've knocked
but as it turns out
you don't like cookies
which is to say
no sale here

rejection
is hard for a little girl to take
i guess that's why
i'm taking it *so hard*

but there's always another day
there's always another sale
and there's always
another product

you may not like my cookies
but have you tried my brownies
you're in for a fucking treat

five dates is cool with me

one hundred forty-four. leash.

finding quality road trip partners
is damn near *impossible*
you have to find someone
who shares your taste in music
someone who makes for
great conversation
and someone who can sleep through
your fucking chainsaw snoring
here's to those people

i have the strangest relationship
with a writer named leash
we barely talk
and i mean barely
we met online years ago
when we were like sixteen
on livejournal of all places
we met once for beer
and we hit it off
and literally
the second time we ever spent time together
we road tripped up the california coast
and it just *worked*

some people just connect
and there's this old soul feeling
almost like
your hearts already know each other
and your brains are playing catch up

one hundred forty-five. savior.

my eyelids are heavy
weighed down by grief
exhaustion
and pseudointellectual bullshit
(among other things)
worst
but most important
of all
my eyelids refuse to open
they want to stay shut
forever
it may be sad
but do not weep
because forever
is only as long
as we believe it is

don't fight it any longer
let the grief overtake you
let your dreams pull you under
lull you softly
and menacingly
let them be the death of you
at least until the sun rises
and you become the savior of tomorrow

one hundred forty-six. i.

late nights
dozens of them
hundreds even
all filled with
distant dreams
and autocorrectly
the age of technology
the age of the i
phones
pads
and pods

what does it say
about us as people
when we can't find
the right words
but our phones can

one hundred forty-seven. turning tables.

drifting slowly
somewhere between
where i am
and where my mind
wants to be
in my dreams
a life far different
far away
from the shit we call reality
don't mind me
i'll be lost here
in between
what is
and what could be
it's the only place i can be with you

half awake
better yet
half asleep
everything at peace
until the day begins
and my mind realizes
my heart plays tricks in my dreams
but soon
reality will turn the tables
my heart will ache
when i wake to see
you are not there
you never were

one hundred forty-eight. a writer's thank you note.

useless
that's how i feel

after all that happened between us
you left me here alone

maybe that's okay
i like being alone

or maybe
i've just gotten used to it

learning to be happy being alone
is the most important thing
because you never know
when you'll find yourself alone
wishing you were with someone
who will never love you back

a sad truth
that *you* made me face

and even though i'm angry and sad and crazy and hollow
i'm also *thankful*
because without you
and without this pain
i may never have had the chance
to get to know myself
and finally find happiness

one hundred forty-nine. playing into the joke.

i like to think
that i'm a pretty funny guy
i have a good sense of humor
and i appreciate a good joke
and from time to time
when someone tells a good joke
and i mean a really, *really* good joke
a joke *so good*
it brings you to tears laughing so hard
and when that someone tells a good joke
specifically a good joke *at my expense*
if it's within my power to play into the joke
to "accidentally" hit myself in the face with something
when someone tells a joke about how dumb i am
or to shove an entire piece of cake in my mouth
when someone tells a joke about how fat i am
i *absolutely* will do what it takes
to get the laugh
do it for the lols
as they say

but what i *hate*
more than anything
is when people assume that i'm not joking
like my actions *aren't* deliberate

okay the cake thing might not have been for the lols
i *really* like cake

one hundred fifty. a real dilemma, humorously.

i love you, man
what a quality movie
what i like best about it
is it's eerily accurate depiction
of what it's like
trying to make friends as an adult
in high school it was easy
you spent all day around the same people
you were forced to see them
why not make it easier and more fun
by turning this in your favor
but as an adult
it's much harder
as a straight man
every woman i try to befriend
thinks i want in her pants
and every man i try and befriend
thinks i want in his pants
much better than how woman have it
every guy they try to befriend
wants in their pants
and every girl they try to befriend
well that generally works out for them
but still
dealing with men who want to sleep with you
has got to be way more frustrating
than anything straight men have to deal with
but i digress
my point is

making friends is hard
no matter what the circumstances
and that movie
definitely illustrates that point
in a realistic yet hilarious way

i think
people should be more clear
about their intentions
if you're trying to befriend someone
you should be able to say
"i find you enjoyable to be around
and i wish to form a platonic attachment"

so the next time
you meet someone
and you think to yourself
"dude
this guy is cool *as fuck*
we should be homies
and do rad shit together"
just say that exact thing out loud
otherwise
you'll end up like
forty five years old or some shit
with no friends
and nobody to be the best man or maid of honor
at your wedding
and that's just sad
(well it's not *that* sad
you *are* getting married after all)

one hundred fifty-one. with or without the life debt.

one of the best things in life
is having a best friend
nobody knows you like they do
solo and chewy
martin and lewis
those two dudes from that road to el dorado cartoon movie
consider yourself lucky if you have a best friend
i consider myself the luckiest bastard
because i have *so many*

smithy
my lover
my composer
and my partner
true love in the form of friendship
never felt so good
you are
a light in my life
the bloom to my bialystock
and i will treasure you
always

of course
there's ralphie
my little jew
with the voice of an angel
who somehow isn't jewish
a true magical singing tree

clark bar
the twenty speed fighter
the little man
with a big heart
double d&d
beer, bosoms, and beholders
the wise hermit
the white knight
who helped me
when no one else could

weisses
though our friendship
more recently
has been rocky
there was a time
the worst of times in fact
that you were there
even when i pushed everyone away
and i'll never be able
to thank you

the duke of earl
a partner
a mentor
and occasionally
a friendly rival
you have never given up on me
even when
i had given up on myself

great scott
fellow soul man
you bearded bastard
we started out
as less than friendly
but with time
and mutual respect
look where we're at

beckstead
you bastard
the brian chewbacca
to my peter griffin han solo
a good bro
an even better man

brian anderson
gone but not forgotten
you were
no, you *are* and always will be
close to my heart

bbq beef
tri tip
oh bricksauce
my dear bricksauce
we go ham
then board the struggle bus
you were my best man
because you
are one of the best men i know

i know i can't talk about
your time in the sas in serbia
working directly for putin
and i know
under no circumstances
am i allowed to talk about
that time you thwarted that nuclear launch in north korea
so i guess i'll just *briefly* mention
that time you rescued bruno the bear from the circus
you fought off twelve rabid clowns and an angry ringleader
man
i miss bruno the bear
you should have never taken him water skiing

one hundred fifty-two. goode times.

you
we gave each other
three fucking years of our lives
that's nothing
to take lightly
i remember
every moment
and yet
looking back
those three years
seem like forever ago

being with you
always felt so easy
so why is
writing about you
so fucking hard to do

we weren't perfect
nobody is
but we
were far from it
sometimes
i think back
and i try to understand
how we stayed together for so long
it seems like such an
impossible thought these days
us together

we met once
before we met
that doesn't make any sense
but it does to you
we met briefly
exchanged hellos
you say you knew then
that we would end up together
i said that too
we both sounded sincere
but i suspect
one of us said it
simply because the other one did
but it's been so long
i don't remember who said it first

it would be years
until we reconnected
we were both older
but we hadn't changed
still the same smile
still the same attraction
although this time
it was *much* stronger
you auditioned for me
and i called you back
you're talented
but casting you was the furthest thing from my mind
all i could think about
was what you said to me
after you auditioned

"your monologue is touching
i hope we get to work together"
and i said
i knew for certain
that i'd be calling you back
you said
"i look forward to it"
and you winked
okay
you didn't wink
but i imagined that you did
and you would later say
you wish you had

later that night
it was almost ten
i called you
just to let you know
i wanted you to come back
for a second audition
and then
suddenly
"hey, can i hang up and call you right back?"
you said
"uh sure"
so i did
and the reason
which you knew
was that i try not to
mix business with pleasure
i had called you as a director

it didn't feel right
trying to connect with you
on a personal level
under the pretext of business
so i hung up
and redialed
and there we were
i guess you could say
the rest
is history

you were unavailable
with a guy
who didn't treat you right
you were unhappy
everyone could tell
but i didn't say anything
because back then
i was respectful
back then
i understood boundaries
friends it was
at least for awhile
you would later confess
that you were crazy about me
and that you wanted
more than anything
to be with me
but you had him
and you would have felt guilty
leaving him to be with me

understandable
that wasn't what *i* wanted
i was crazy about you too
you could tell
everyone could tell
but the last thing i wanted
was to be the cause
of your heartbreak

three weeks we endured
you fought with him
almost every day
by your account
and almost every day
i thought of you
but i put that thought
out of my mind
thinking that
the day would never come
but then
you called me
you asked to see me
i agreed
we went to in'n'out
i still have the photos
nothing seemed different
i think that was the point
we talked and we laughed
and things were goode
and then
on the car ride back to your place

you said it
"i broke up with him"
i thought you were joking
i smiled and i laughed
but you didn't
you were serious
and to this day
i'll always feel terrible
for what i said
"finally"
we were both relieved
but you didn't show it
not that night

the next night
we sat outside your best friend's house
in my dad's truck
and all we did was talk
about him
about you
about us
we spent hours in the truck
just like we always did
we would spend hours sitting and talking
goode times
but that night
that night we talked openly
for the first time
you told me how you felt
i couldn't breathe
the first time in recorded history that i was speechless

i started to tell you
how i felt about you
but you knew
you always knew
and then
i'll never forget
for as long as i live
that moment
i made that face
i *always* make
and you made that face
you always make
and you leaned in
and kissed me
we kissed
and it was goode

things were goode
for awhile
but nothing lasts forever
or so they say
we fought
we fought *a lot*
about the smallest things
but the picture
that was the turning point
you trusted me
despite everyone's warning
you trusted me
and i lied
and things were never the same

as the years passed
we grew apart
and though
i recall every detail
every fight
every break
none of it is important
but what *is*
is that through it all
through all the pain
and jealousy
the love remained
and i think you'd agree
that that
is what made it so difficult
we could handle the fights
and the accusations
we could handle the screaming
and we even handled
being stopped by the campus police
because someone saw us fighting
and feared for *my* safety
we both got a kick out of that
but we handled all of it
but the one thing we couldn't handle
was still loving each other
was knowing we still loved each other
and watching ourselves
slowly and surely
fall out of love
and suddenly it wasn't goode anymore

these days
i find myself thinking about
you and i
as we were
all those years ago
wondering if
we could *ever* recapture
what we had
when we were younger
you said we couldn't
though i disagree
perhaps that proves your point
but i'll *always*
have hope
for us

the sun is setting now
and as the moon rises to greet the night sky
i am reminded
of the love affair
of prince moonlight and princess sunshine
doomed to a life apart
the morning sun
and the evening moon
perhaps you're right after all
perhaps there *is no* hope for them
but alas
every so often
you can spy the moon during the day
stealing a warm embrace
from the lover he could never have

one hundred fifty-three. in remembrance.

gone but not forgotten
never forget that
those of you
who have lost
friends or family
or both
they are gone but *not* forgotten
no matter what you believe
a part of them
is always with us
our memories of them
the experiences we shared with them
the lives they touched
there are pieces of them
all around us
you just have to
close your eyes and feel them
they are there
with us
you can feel them, can't you
beside you when you succeed
behind you pushing when you struggle
comforting you when you fail
inspiring you to brush yourself off and try again
they are there
they love you
and they are *proud*
gone but *not* forgotten
never forget that

246

one hundred fifty-four. devil's parody.

i get lonely sometimes
not because i'm alone
but because nobody gets the joke
*"once you realize what a joke everything is
being the comedian is the only thing that makes sense"*
words of a man
who has distanced himself
from his humanity
desensitized
society expects so much
and when it becomes too much
you have to cut away your humanity
to be able to give people what they *need*
and sometimes what they need
is to be shown an extreme
to demonstrate what they could become
if they don't save themselves
*"look at what you've done
look at what you could become"*
some people choose to be that parody
i call it the devil's parody
because sometimes people need that
people need those extremes
to help them form their own opinions
to help them strengthen their beliefs
it's a hard thing to do
to be that parody
but it gets easier
the more jaded you become

and unsurprisingly
i think i know what you're thinking
you're thinking
"being an asshole
claiming it's to help people
that's a cop out
it's just an excuse
to allow you to be an asshole
it's an afterthought
some thrown together excuse
to try and cover up the fact
that you're just an asshole"
and i would agree with you
most of the time
there are people out there
who are *just* assholes
for no other reason
than because they are assholes
but i think that on occasion
you'll find someone
who has an acute understanding of human nature
someone like the comedian
who lives life as an extreme
so that others can see
what they will suffer through
what they will become
and hopefully
they change
they become a better person
hopefully
here's hoping

248

"we do what we have to do
the comedian understood
treated it like a joke
but he understood
he saw the cracks in society
he saw the true face of the twentieth century
chose to become a reflection of it
a parody of it
no one else saw the joke
that's why he was lonely"
and that's why i'm lonely
because no one else sees the joke

a devil's parody
that's how i choose to live
choosing to be something
someone
that people can learn from
even if i have to be an example
of what *not* to become
maybe it's because
i'm beyond saving
and i'm using
what last shred of decency i have left in me
to give others
what i'll *never* be able to have myself

"i didn't say it was a good joke
i'm just playing along with the gag"

the divine spark
the power to bring
joy and happiness
to those around you

that's all well and good
but what about pain
anger
and sorrow
i'm not saying we need more of those
there's enough chaos and despair in this life
we could definitely use
a lot more positivity
my problem is
this divine spark paints the picture that
only joy and happiness can help people
who decided
that sadness needed to stand in a circle
and read a technical manual
while joy took the wheel

as a writer
i don't have this divine spark
i might occasionally make people laugh
or put a smile on their face
but my work is filled with despair
it's filled with anger and suffering
but that's not a bad thing
these emotions aren't morally bad emotions

these emotions can help
opening peoples' hearts and minds is divine
and that can be done by sharing your pain
and your fear
and your suffering
helping people deal with their own shit
that's divine
comforting someone through loss is divine
even if it means sharing your own loss

now i understand
that the idea of the divine spark
is just some movie trope
used in sappy comedy movies
like where a man is given the power of god
i get it
but it's important to remember
that life is more than
smiles and cupcakes and rainbows
life is shit
sometimes bad shit happens
most people don't deal with the death of a loved one
by cracking a few jokes and slipping on a banana peel
real people get angry
real people cry and then get angry again
real people break stuff and ugly cry
and then regret breaking that stuff when they're standing in
line at best buy buying a new set of studio headphones
because fuck why did i break those fucking headphones
do you think
that a mother of three

who works two jobs
struggling to pay the bills and make ends meat
is going to laugh when
the pharmacist filling her prescriptions
mixes up the medication
and then cracks a joke about not being paid enough
to try and lighten the mood
no
just
no

look
i know i'm taking this whole thing
way too seriously
but maybe
you aren't taking it seriously enough

some people
craft stories filled with joy
to brighten the lives of others
and some people
craft stories filled with pain
to help others cope with their own
to me
that should carry equal weight

the divine spark
the power to bring
comfort and aid
to those around you

one hundred fifty-six. inevitability.

one of the saddest things in the world
is the death of romanticism
some people seem to think
that blindly holding out for the right person
your prince charming
your princess lovely
your unicorn
is stupid
or that making mix tapes
or origami flowers
is stupid
why
why is it stupid
to think that there is someone out there
who will appreciate your effort
who *deserves* your effort
i think what's stupid
is telling someone their romanticism is stupid
what's stupid
is telling someone they're too cheesy
or that their romanticism is hopeless
there's nothing hopeless about true love
hopelessness is letting your broken heart stay broken
hopelessness is waiting for someone else
to fix your broken heart *for* you
true love isn't *hopeless*
it's inevitable

one hundred fifty-seven. relate.

driving home late at night
after a long day
i sometimes feel my eyelids
weighed down by exhaustion
and there i am
behind the wheel

next thing i know
i'm sitting in front of my apartment
perfectly parked
with *no fucking idea*
how i got there

sometimes i get that way
in relationships
there i am
arm around a beautiful girl
next thing i know
i'm sitting in front of my apartment
perfectly parked
with *no fucking idea*
why we broke up

life is like that sometimes
you can relate
can't you

one hundred fifty-eight. a love note for my ex-wife.

to the love
of my life
yes *you*, my dear
i write you this note
much too late
in hopes
that you will see
how much
i *love* you

i love you
more than
you love me
we used to argue that point
i remember
you used to say
you loved me more
than you loved yourself
and i *know* you loved yourself

i love you
more than
you love big black dicks
no need to argue that point
i remember
you used to say
you'd never cheat
that you loved me too much
but i *know* that was a lie

i love you
more than
you hate my friends
there's no arguing that point
i remember
you used to demand
i give up my friends
to give you all my love
and i *know* you hated that i didn't

but i know you loved me
in your own way
at least for a little while
maybe at first
when the sex was good
and things were equal
the way you said you wanted them
you're a feminist after all
you insisted on supporting yourself
you wouldn't accept my money
and that was okay
because you had to be your own person
and i *love* that about you
you did your thing
i did my thing
we had great sex

i *love* you
i love you so much
but i can't love you anymore
i *shouldn't* love you anymore

but it's been hard
getting over you
that sounds crazy
you cheated
you lied about me to your family
you did everything in your power
to convince me *i* was crazy
to make *me* look like the bad guy
but i wasn't the bad guy
you were
but
i was weak
i was weak and i loved you
(a terrible combination)
and even though i wasn't the bad guy
i played the part
you lied about me to your family
and then i would apologize to you in front of them
to make you look good
and accept all your blame
but that's okay
because i loved you
wait
did i say *loved*
i meant *love*
shit
maybe i *did* mean loved
maybe
it's hard to tell
through all the pain
and all the tears

i *loved* you
more than
you loved me
you won't argue that point anymore
i remember
you used to say
you loved me
more than you loved yourself
but i *know* that isn't true anymore

i don't blame *you*
i blame *myself*
because what you *didn't* know
what *nobody* knew
is that i loved someone else
someone from a long time ago
someone who will never love me back
and i thought
i could move on
i thought
i could love someone else
but i was wrong
you stopped trying
you cheated
that's on *you*
but *i* loved someone else
and that's on *me*

i *did* love you
but you weren't her
nobody will *ever* be her

one hundred fifty-nine. the truth, painfully.

time for a confession
a *brutally honest* confession
from the lips of a charming liar
who loved many women
but never *himself*
and who touched many souls
but never *his own*
he is empty
and yearning
he knows he'll never be whole
he knows he'll always be half
but he tries
and he tries
to fill the void
to find the other half
to find the piece he is missing
but he tries
and he fails
so he tries
and he tries
to love himself as he is
to experience himself
and embrace his soul
but despite all his efforts
he still comes up short
lacking
unfulfilled
he drowns himself with his fancies
he drowns himself in love

in lust
in hopeless romanticism
he hides within other people's souls
touches them softly
and sweetly
but he shouldn't
not when he's like this
not when he isn't whole
because when he's like this
and he touches their soul
he takes a part of them
he steals a piece for himself
to fix his own soul
and when he does
they suffer
and then they're wounded
incomplete
just like him
he's a disease
infecting everyone he touches
some of them stay
and it isn't pretty
they don't realize what he has done
so it continues
and they lose more and more of themselves
he takes what's good in them
and leaves them bitter
angry
and empty
all while he patches himself up
and moves on thinking he's okay

but he's not
and everyone knows it
even he knows
deep down he knows
but he pretends
hoping it'll help
but it doesn't
because *nobody*
will make him whole again
only he can do that
some people realize that
some people see through him
the people that do
those that realize what he's doing
those that realize what he has done
they leave
hoping
they can fix themselves
wishing
more than anything
that they could hurt him
for what he has done
for the pain he has caused
for the damage he has done
but somehow
they don't
they *want* to
but they don't
because they also realize
he's already hurt
much worse

than what they could ever do to him
and for them
that's enough
it *has* to be
because they don't *ever* want to be like him

and that's the truth
the *brutally honest* truth
from the heart of a broken boy
who lied to many people
including himself
who hurt many souls
especially his own

one hundred sixty. your turn.

acknowledgments.

People always ask if I've written about them, and the answer is always yes.

I promised myself that the first person I would always acknowledge is my dad, Randy Campbell, without whom I would not be who I am today. Everything I do, I do to make him proud.

To my family and friends: thank you. You have stood by me through everything and you've dragged me through the mud when I deserved it.

To my ex-wife, my ex-girlfriends, and all the other women I've been with: I'm sorry. I've never been a good man and you've all suffered because of it.

To my haters, my enemies, and those who generally wish bad juju upon me: you're right. I've lied, scammed, and bullshitted my way through life. But on the other hand: *go fuck yourself.*

Important people worth mentioning by name: Ulrike Sachse-Campbell, Mikey Kaufman, Joann Slaughter, Ali Scurlock, Liz Cadigan, Mikey Chavez, Laura Seese, Ora Barbabosa, Lauren Stanford, Amanda Kincaid, Courtney Clegg, Madison Kaleigh Jerles, Amber Goode, John and Estee Anderson, Duke Delaet, Scott Donohue, Christopher Clark, Jon Maguire, Pierre Alexander Smith, Brandon Lang, Patrick Beckstead, Grant Goldstein, Warner Salisbury, Jack Hoskinson, Edward Brecht, Austin Luther, Christi Watson, David Rathaus, Rob Gzyl, Jenea Huston, Sam Fisher, Ashley Shahamiri, Brianna LaCanfora, and, of course, tumblr.

And finally, thank *you*. You know who you are.